S0-BDP-707

RAISING CONFIDENT HAPPY CHILDREN

RAISING CONFIDENT HAPPY CHILDREN

40 ways to help your child succeed

ANTHONY GUNN

hardie grant books
MELBOURNE · LONDON

IPSWICH LIBRARY & INFORMATION SERVICE

Published in Australia in 2010 by
Hardie Grant Books
85 High Street
Prahran, Victoria 3181, Australia
www.hardiegrant.com.au

Published in the United Kingdom in 2010 by
Hardie Grant Books (London)

All rights reserved. No part of this publication may be reproduced,
stored in a retrieval system or transmitted in any form by any means,
electronic, mechanical, photocopying, recording or otherwise, without
the prior written permission of the publishers and copyright holders.

The moral rights of the author have been asserted.

Copyright © Anthony Gunn 2010

National Library of Australia Cataloguing-in-Publication data:
Gunn, Anthony, 1975–
   Raising confident, happy children / Anthony Gunn.
   ISBN 9781740667494 (pbk.)
   Child rearing. Confidence in children. Happiness in children.
   Child psychology.
649.7

Cover and internal design by Natalie Winter
Typeset by Megan Ellis
Cover photograph courtesy of Getty Images
Printed and bound in Australia by McPherson's Printing Group

10 9 8 7 6 5 4 3 2 1

To my two beautiful children, Emma and Patrick

CONTENTS

INTRODUCTION

'One generation plants the trees;
another gets the shade.'

CHINESE PROVERB

Why is confidence so important for a child? Research shows that a confident child is more likely to have a happy and successful life. A child who believes in their own ability is more likely to succeed at school than a child with natural ability who lacks belief in themselves. Children who are certain of their abilities are reported to be more curious and to participate in, enjoy and persist at school tasks more. Children who are uncertain of their own abilities are more likely to lose interest in school, avoid getting involved in activities, feel anxious, angry and bored, and have a decline in their academic performance. The take-home message here is clear: you may be missing a vital factor in your child's mental wellbeing if you don't nurture and build your child's confidence.

Parenting is hard work, contrary to what the media and Hollywood stars might say. Studies show that when a person becomes a parent, their anxiety levels skyrocket. Why is this? Take your pick: sleepless nights, lack of free time to do your own thing, attending to your child's injuries or taking them to medical appointments, running around after them for sport/swimming/music lessons, dealing with temper tantrums, coping with bullying by other children, social issues – your child has no friends or mixes with the wrong friends, inappropriate clothes, messy bedrooms, no desire to go to school, listening to loud or inappropriate music. Parenting is anxiety-provoking, hard work!

It may not seem normal or fair that parents should experience this level of anxiety. But while it isn't fair, it *is* normal, and it has a positive function. Anxiety is nature's way of ensuring that parents protect their child from harm. Part of this protection involves carefully teaching a child to stand on their own two feet. This might seem counter-intuitive, but helping your child develop confidence involves standing back and watching them step out of comfort zones. This requires courage on your part; the more confident and courageous your child becomes, the more courageous you will have to be to support their growth.

This balancing act between being overprotective and being careless with your child's safety is one that causes many parents grief. If letting go and allowing your child to step out of comfort zones is an issue for you, you can feel safe in the knowledge that you're normal. Not only will this book teach you how to help your child develop their confidence, but it will also give you, the parent, strategies for coping as you watch your child's confidence increase.

Most importantly, these parenting strategies come without a guilt trip. All parents feel guilt because all parents make mistakes. Even though I often know the right thing to do as a parent, I don't always apply my own teachings. It might be because I'm focused on other things at the time or simply because I'm tired. We're human and parenting is difficult; no one has mastered it. But if we have guidelines for how to parent effectively, we will be more inclined to do right by our child more often than not. Our focus, therefore, is on looking forward instead of dwelling on the past; this will give your child the best opportunity for building confidence. By offering some new ideas about parenting, or perhaps just reminding you of the ones you've forgotten, this book will help you manage your guilt and debunk the idea of the perfect parent so that you can do the best by your child.

Who should read this book?

Throughout this book I use the word 'parent'. However, this book will also be helpful for teachers, coaches, family members, guardians and any other adult who deals with children. So when you see the word *parent*, apply whichever term works for you.

How should you use this book?

Children learn by watching other people. Whether you are a parent, guardian, grandparent, family member, teacher, coach or friend, as an adult you are in a powerful position to help build the confidence and happiness of the child in your care by being a positive role model. You achieve this by modelling to your child how to do the exercises in this book. It's best if you follow the forty tips in order as the exercises build on previous chapters. As children are great at copying, you will be modelling not only how to do the exercise but also how to respond emotionally – happily and confidently. Rest assured, you'll be taught how!

The set exercises for parents

You'll find some exercises that are specifically for parents to do without the child present. These exercises are not designed to flood you with guilt about your parenting, but rather to help develop and refine your role modelling skills. Make sure you resist the temptation to overlook these exercises and only do the ones involving your child. By developing your own skills, you are building on potentially the most important principle of all, that children learn by watching other people.

When using any of the exercises or suggestions outlined in this book, keep in mind the following basic rules:

* **START GRADUALLY** Begin by stepping out of small comfort zones first; too big a step too quickly usually results in shattered confidence.

* **HAVE FUN** Treat all the exercises, where possible, like a game. Children (and adults) learn much better when having fun.

* **LISTEN TO YOUR CHILD** When a child doesn't feel listened to or understood, their confidence suffers. Take the time to listen to your child's concerns and go at their pace as this provides a sense of security for them.

* **NORMALISE FEAR** It's normal to feel fear or discomfort when stepping out of a comfort zone. If a child, or an adult for that matter, didn't feel fear in these situations, then they wouldn't be comfort zones.

* **PRAISE YOUR CHILD** Any time your child takes a step towards their goal, no matter how small, praise them. This will motivate them to continue taking steps forward.

What age group does the book cater for?

This book is written for school-age children, predominantly primary-school age, five to twelve years. It's harder to use the cognitive (thinking) strategies outlined in the book with children below this age as they generally won't yet have the brain development to understand the tasks. The techniques can be used with teenagers, but I recommend reading up about adolescent development so you can apply the techniques in an adolescent-friendly way. Adolescence is all about developing autonomy, so treating a sixteen-year-old as you would an eight-year-old could risk either an argument or crushed confidence.

How do I know if my child needs professional help?

Some of the tips in this book will help with childhood psychological disorders, but you might still need to seek professional help. The simple way to determine if your child needs professional help is whether the issue is affecting both their and your everyday life. For example, if every time you take your child to school it is a traumatic event or they are considerably more anxious than other children their age, or if your child's excessive anxiety has been present for more than six months, then it's a sign to seek help.

Remember, all children are different. As you go through this book and try the tips, keep those that are helpful and dismiss those that are not. However, let your child's response to the tasks determine whether an activity is helpful. Try an activity at least twice before dismissing it. You will have to experience a degree of discomfort for your confidence levels to increase. Experiencing discomfort in small, gradual and realistic steps is the key to building confidence.

Now, let's get started in building your child's confidence and, in turn, their happiness.

1

STRETCH THE RULES

*'I try not to break the rules, but
merely to test their elasticity.'*

BILL VEECK

For the school holidays, Steve had purchased a new inflatable sled to tow behind his ski-boat for his seven-year-old son, James, to ride on. Steve, his wife and James were staying at a caravan park next to a large lake. One morning all three of them hopped into the boat and sped out into the middle of the lake. Steve then turned the boat off, threw the inflatable sled out and attached it to the rear of the boat. In Steve's mind, James would simply hold on to the sled while Steve towed him around the lake. There was one problem Steve hadn't envisaged, however: James froze upon seeing the deep water and said he wasn't strong enough to hold on to the sled without falling off. Steve got annoyed; he knew that once James got out there he'd love it. But the more Steve pressured, the more convinced James became that he couldn't handle the sled. Eventually Steve yelled in frustration, James burst into tears and James's mother told her husband not to push him any further. The day was a disaster.

What is it that allows some children to try new things, but drives other children to avoid them? Psychologists would likely say that James has low self-efficacy in regards to being towed behind his father's boat. What is self-efficacy? It is the belief a person holds about their capability and confidence to perform when faced with a difficult task. Children low in self-efficacy become anxious when they perceive themselves as ill-equipped or unable to handle potentially threatening situations. Children high in self-efficacy are more likely to attempt new behaviours and persist with those behaviours until mastered, thereby increasing chances of success. Research suggests that high self-efficacy may predict positive development in childhood and protect against anxiety and depression.

It's important not to confuse the term self-efficacy with self-esteem. Self-efficacy relates to a person's perception about their ability to reach a goal, whereas self-esteem relates to a person's sense of self-worth. So even though James may have poor self-efficacy with regard to his ability to hold on to the sled, this need not affect his self-esteem if he doesn't see the activity as important. Both self-esteem and self-efficacy are very important for a child's confidence and happiness levels, yet it's self-efficacy that will largely determine whether they choose to step out of a comfort zone and try a new task.

How would you know if your child has low self-efficacy? Common signs are all based on a child avoiding situations that they perceive as threatening. Some examples of this avoidance include:

* **LACK OF INTERACTION** Standing back and not interacting or making new friends at social events, such as parties, team sports, school or during play dates with friends. It's normal for a child to be initially reserved until they feel comfortable with their new surroundings, but once they do, they should interact.

* **MAKING EXCUSES** Coming up with excuses to avoid certain situations, for example, pretending to feel sick on the day they have to give a speech in class.

* **LACK OF INTEREST** Appearing uninterested in a task they feel they could never master: 'I don't want to do drawing in class because it's boring.' (Be aware, though, that if a task is either too challenging or not

challenging enough it can create a lack of interest in the child.)

* **TANTRUMS** A child may react angrily if faced with confronting something they fear they can't handle, for instance, a child with a learning difficulty being expected to function like all the other children, or a child with school phobia being forced to attend school. This anger is known as the fight or flight response to danger.

So how can you help develop your child's self-efficacy? You can start by teaching them about unwritten rules, especially the unwritten rules they apply to their abilities.

Self-imposed rules

Our lives are governed by rules. Many of these rules protect us from harm – road rules, for example. If people didn't follow road rules and instead drove on whichever side of the road they wanted, things would get ugly very quickly. But some rules don't prevent us from harm. Rather, they prevent us from feeling confident, pushing boundaries and achieving success. These are the rules we place upon ourselves about what we cannot do, and they are rarely, if ever, questioned. Perhaps they should be.

Self-imposed rules we hold about ourselves can be illustrated by the person who says:

* I'm just naturally shy, which is why I could never be involved in positions of importance, like being on a committee.

* My child is like me and doesn't have an original/ sporting/dancing bone in their body.

* I'm no good with handling the kids' emotional needs; I leave that to my wife.

* I've never been taught how to cook, which is why I rely on takeaway or frozen meals.

* I would love to exercise and look after my health, but I just don't have the time.

The list of rules above will differ from person to person and is far from definitive. Generally these rules are taken as absolute truths and we wouldn't dream of testing their accuracy. Yet when a self-imposed rule is tested and stretched, even just a little, it's virtually impossible for it to maintain its original hold over a person.

Build your child's self-efficacy to stretch self-imposed rules

The trouble is that, like adults, children often believe that their self-imposed rules are keeping them safe. Overly anxious children believe that avoiding the things that make them feel anxious actually protects them. In reality, trying to avoid feeling anxiety only makes the anxiety worse and keeps a child prisoner to their comfort zones. This is why the hardest part of encouraging a child to stretch any self-imposed rule is teaching them that they can handle the associated anxiety.

How do you help your child believe that they can manage the discomfort associated with stretching self-imposed rules? Start by encouraging your child to stretch smaller rules in their life that don't provoke anxiety. This will build their confidence to then test their more unhelpful and anxiety-provoking self-imposed rules.

Together with your child, start building self-efficacy by stretching the following smaller, less threatening unwritten rules. Make your child aware of the associated discomfort that comes with stretching the rules, and praise them for being able to manage it.

* **DINNER MUST BE EATEN A SET WAY.** Eat dinner with your cutlery in the opposite hands or with chopsticks.

* **EVERYONE HAS THEIR SET PLACE.** Swap the seating arrangement if you sit in set places for dinner or when watching television, or, if you're daring, sit under the table while you all have dessert (children love this).

* **ALWAYS USE THE SAME HAND FOR DRAWING.**
  Draw with the non-dominant hand and notice how
  uncomfortable it feels.

* **YOUR BED DOESN'T CHANGE.** Sleep one night with
  your head at the opposite end of the bed.

* **READ FROM START TO FINISH.** Read a short, basic
  picture book backwards, from the end to the start.

* **A PROBLEM HAS ONLY ONE SOLUTION.** Show your
  child more than one solution to a problem, such as
  different ways to tie your shoelaces.

Make a game out of stretching the above rules with your
child, with the emphasis on having fun. Expect your child
to be unsure and to ask questions about why you are
changing everyday rules. Remember, rules give us security,
especially for children. If you can show that unwritten rules,
ones that don't threaten safety, can be stretched without
any major consequences, it will build their self-efficacy to
start changing the rules they've placed on themselves. Take
your time in fostering your child's self-efficacy around
stretching rules. As your child's confidence increases, you
can set them the challenge of stretching their smaller self-
imposed rules. Remember, make it fun and go at your
child's pace, because if you pressure them, your efforts will
be counterproductive.

Examples of self-imposed rules that you could encourage your child to stretch:

* Doing an activity they wouldn't normally do, e.g. indoor rock climbing, a sport or art.

* Feeding or patting an animal they wouldn't normally encounter, e.g. at a zoo or animal nursery for children.

* Visiting a place they wouldn't normally visit, e.g. a lookout or a destination that requires a plane, train or boat ride.

Summing up

Our lives are governed by rules, rules that are there for our own safety. However, the rules we place on ourselves about what we can't do are generally both misleading and harmful. By stretching self-imposed rules, you are testing their credibility, thereby decreasing their stranglehold. When a child believes they can manage the anxiety associated with stretching a self-imposed rule, they are in a better position to try new challenges in life. This will make them less susceptible to the negative impacts of anxiety and depression.

As you read through the tips in this book and apply the practical exercises to both yourself and your child, keep in mind the issue of self-efficacy. By gradually going at your child's pace, you will be fostering high self-efficacy. And it's self-efficacy that is the key to unlocking your child's confidence to face new challenges and try new things. High self-efficacy helps a child believe they can achieve.

2

KNOW YOUR CHILD'S BRAIN

*'If the human brain were so simple
that we could understand it, we would
be so simple that we couldn't.'*

EMERSON M. PUGH

How far back in your childhood can you remember? Put down the book and try it now.

How did you go? Studies show that when adults are asked to recall their earliest childhood memories, recollections typically date back no further than age three or four. The reason is that prior to this age the part of the brain responsible for long-term memory isn't properly formed.

The human brain is an amazingly powerful and unique part of the body. Did you know that the brain makes up only 2 per cent of the body's mass but uses a massive 20 per cent of its energy? Even though 75 per cent of adult brain weight is attained by the age of two, the brain keeps growing until approximately age twenty-five. It's this final quarter of growth, after two years of age, that is largely responsible for things like memory, reasoning and problem-solving skills, and understanding one's own emotions. This is why a young child will not have the intellect to comprehend many everyday things, especially things that scare them. Yet, many adults expect a young child to see the world as they do and, when the child can't, the adult gets annoyed.

When Olivia first went to school, she cried as her mum prepared to leave her. Olivia's mum snapped at her, telling her to stop being a baby and to grow up. Olivia was five years old, and she was terrified that if she let her mum go, she would be taken by angels, like her grandfather had been. Because Olivia's granddad died in his sleep without any warning, Olivia blamed herself that she wasn't there to stop the angels from taking him away. Her situation was made even more terrifying and confusing because while she was trying to save her mum from being taken by the angels, her mum was punishing her for it. It was Olivia's teacher who found out the truth. She had become concerned by Olivia's anxious behaviour and loss of appetite during the day. Once the teacher reassured Olivia that angels wouldn't take her mother, and helped correct her distorted beliefs around death, Olivia started acting like her usual self again.

Olivia's mum had dismissed her daughter's fears as attention-seeking and used the tough love approach, expecting her to get over it. The 'get over it' approach doesn't offer any explanation to the cause of a fear, and it can be terrifying for a child. This is because a child's brain is still developing, which often prevents them from accurately seeing how cause and effect works in life as an adult can. Olivia's granddad died because of a heart attack, not because angels dragged him away. When a child is expected to grow into shoes that are too big, the oversized shoes can make the child appear clumsy and awkward. It is the same with a child's brain. As the child grows into their brain they will also appear clumsy and awkward, and have troubles making sense of their world.

Brain development can be seen in children's reactions to certain situations or stimuli based on their age. One way of seeing this is in the way children progressively fear definite things as they grow older. This is Mother Nature's way of keeping a child safe.

* From birth, an infant only has two fears – falling and loud noises.

* At six months of age, or when the child starts to crawl, the fear of heights and water develops for their own protection.

* From approximately six to nine months of age, a fear of strangers develops.

* Around two years of age, the time a child is able to be more adventurous, a fear of animals, especially snakes and spiders, starts.

* At approximately three years of age, a child's imagination develops. This brain function allows them to predict future danger so they can avoid it: 'If I touch the flame of the birthday-cake candle, I'll get burnt.' However, this imagination also causes nightmares and a fear of the dark, such as monsters under the bed.

As a child's brain becomes more developed, so too does their ability to apply reason to their environmental fears. Psychologists claim that when a child can apply reason to their innate fears and feel they have a sense of control over them, the child is able to successfully conquer these fears. For example, if a child is able to climb to the top of a slippery dip and then slide down, this suggests that the fear of heights has been mastered. However, when a child can't put a logical reason to the particular fear and gain a sense of control over it, the child becomes unable to outgrow and move on from that fear. This can be seen with many adult phobias, which are often childhood fears that were never outgrown.

However, it's not just innate fears that highlight the way a child's brain develops. The ability to stay focused on a specific task is another area of interest. Research shows that a child's ability to sustain attention improves between the ages of one and four, but most four-year-olds still have a hard time focusing on a task for very long. Between the ages of five and twelve, children are still improving their ability to filter out irrelevant input, such as being able to focus on a story being read to them while ignoring the noise in the background. But ask any primary school teacher the difference between a kindergarten child's ability to concentrate on a story and a sixth grade student's and they'll tell you that the differences are vast. This level of ability to maintain attention is why it can be so frustrating trying to get a young child to sit down and do the same activity for a long period of time.

Without an appreciation of a child's psychological limitations, parents can fall into the trap of unknowingly pushing their child to face fears in life the child isn't mentally equipped for. How then can you be mindful of your child's developing brain so that their development isn't disadvantaged? Start by being respectful of your child's fears and encouraging them to talk to you about their worries and concerns. Even though their fears may seem odd, illogical or crazy, they are still very real to your child. By showing empathy and understanding instead of the 'get over it' approach, you are in a better position to help encourage and support your child to gradually face their fears. Remember, Mother Nature gives us fears for a reason – protection. This is especially true for children. So be patient in helping your child develop the belief, or self-efficacy, that they can conquer their fears.

Even with the most perfect of intentions, a parent is still trying to see their child's fears through adult eyes. It can be highly beneficial to learn to see your child's fear from their view. By seeing life through a child's eyes, a child's fears suddenly make more sense.

Have you ever looked at something from a new angle and noticed how different it appears? Try looking at your house from your neighbour's place, or on Google Maps. Seeing an issue or situation from a different angle can give a whole new perspective. Try one of the following exercises with your child:

* Grip a pen with your fingers and thumb wrapped around the pen, like you're holding a large stick, so the index finger can't be extended forward for support. If held correctly, the pen should be at a ninety-degree angle to the paper. Then try writing your name. This exercise gives an idea of a young child's limited strength and poor hand–eye coordination.

* Close your eyes and have your child lead you around the house, relying solely on their directions to avoid obstacles. This exercise helps highlight what it's like

for a child to be so dependent on their parent to guide them through the obstacles in the world.

* Crouch down and walk around the house at your child's height so you can see what life looks like from their eye level.

Psychologists have long known that when we put ourselves in another person's shoes, we are far more likely to feel empathy for and understanding of their situation. What's more, feeling empathy helps avoid the trap of seeing others' worries and concerns as insignificant. It's one thing just to say we understand being in our child's shoes, but it's altogether different to actually experience it.

Summing up

Give your child the freedom to be clumsy and fearful while they are growing into their brain. When it comes to your child's fears, know that they have been hardwired for their own protection to fear certain things at certain ages. Listen to your child's concerns and acknowledge them without being judgemental. If your child feels listened to and understood, they'll be more inclined to share any other fears that surface in the future. So try walking in your child's shoes and seeing life as their brain sees it.

3

MAKE A GAME OUT OF FEAR

*'Nothing diminishes anxiety
faster than action.'*

WALTER ANDERSON

Should you make a child face their fear and risk exacerbating it? This is the big problem that many parents experience when their child is faced with a new challenge.

Brett had a phobia of balloons and avoided them at all costs. So intense was his fear that if he was invited to a school friend's party, his parents would speak to the friend's parents beforehand and ask that they not have any balloons at the party. This even included Brett's school, which stopped using balloons at the school discos, all for Brett's sake. Brett's parents also made sure that there were no balloons at his aunt's wedding. The end of the school year loomed, when Brett would have to make the transition to high school. Even though Brett was popular at school, his parents held grave concerns for their son's wellbeing once the high school students found out about his fear of balloons.

Every time a phobia is avoided it becomes stronger. In Brett's case, his parents fed his phobia with avoidance each time they made sure social events had no balloons. When this was pointed out to them, they were horrified; by trying to protect their son from fear, they were actually making things worse.

There is a flipside to fear avoidance. If a child is instead pushed into facing a fear that is beyond them, it can actually make the fear worse, as was the case with Sasha.

Sasha was a very gifted twenty-year-old singer but she would not perform in public; instead, she was paid to sing the backing tracks for TV commercials. In her job, she met people from the music industry, many of whom had told her that she had what it takes to be a star. But Sasha would nearly vomit at the thought of performing in front of a crowd. When she was twelve, her father proudly booked her first gig, singing a song at a family wedding. Sasha was so nervous that she pleaded with her father not to go ahead with it, but he refused to listen, saying that everything would be fine. As Sasha nervously walked up on stage, all she could see were two hundred faces watching her. When it came time to sing, she froze, her mind went blank and she forgot her words. After a pause that seemed to last forever, Sasha ran off the stage in tears, totally humiliated. She had faced her fear of singing in public, but it had only made the fear worse. Now, as a result, she was unable to follow her dream of being a performer.

If assisting your child to avoid fear-provoking situations only feeds the fear, as in Brett's case, yet facing fear head-on risks shattering a person's confidence, as in Sasha's case, then what is the answer? Three words – take small steps. It's vital that you encourage your child to step out of comfort zones and face fear, but in small, gradual steps that they can manage so as not to destroy their confidence. Psychologists studying brain function have discovered that if a new situation poses too little fear, or is too safe, then it's unlikely the child will learn anything from it. On the other hand, when a situation poses too much fear, it's unlikely the child will cope, which will result in anxiety and withdrawal from the situation altogether. However, when children are exposed to a fear-provoking situation that they can handle, it lays down the neural foundation in their brain for mastering future threats and helps them find ways to calm themselves down.

The key here is to help your child face fearful situations realistically, at both their pace and level of difficulty. If a child is rushed into facing a fear too quickly and at a level beyond their ability for coping, you risk crushing their confidence. Break down the fear into manageable steps. Take the example of making a speech in public. If this were to be broken down into steps from easiest to hardest then it may look something like this:

1. Write out the speech.
2. Practise the speech:
   a. with no one around.
   b. in front of a mirror.
   c. in front of a video camera.
   d. in front of a trusted person.
   e. in front of a small group of trusted people.
3. Give the speech for real.

When you break down facing a fear into small, manageable steps, you look after a person's confidence. This can be applied to any fear. Many of the examples throughout this book will use this strategy of progressive exposure. Keep an eye out for this strategy's application in other areas. Write down how you could break down facing a fear for your child. Once you start thinking in this way, it becomes a lot easier to do.

Rate discomfort

Once you feel comfortable with breaking down fears into manageable steps, you're ready to help your child with the next step for facing fear: have your child rate their discomfort.

Controlling one's own reaction when stepping out of a comfort zone is one of the best ways of taking charge of a situation. A popular psychology adage says, 'If you can't measure it, you can't manage it'. Having your child rate their discomfort in response to the situation is a very effective way of teaching them to manage their own reaction. Whenever they step out of a comfort zone into an unfamiliar situation, have them rate their discomfort on a scale of one to ten. One represents no discomfort, ten represents extreme discomfort. I'm always amazed at how this simple act of rating discomfort helps give a person a sense of control. The reason it works so well is that it shows them that their anxiety is rarely a ten out of ten, nor does it stay at high levels for long before dropping. The rating scale is especially effective for children because it keeps things simple by avoiding difficult techniques and large, technical words, both of which are easily forgotten when discomfort levels are high.

In order for your child to get maximum effect from the rating scale, they will need to be able to sit with their discomfort long enough to see it drop. The best way to do this is to teach your child to surf their anxiety. This means to stick with it and observe the anxiety until it subsides. Even though anxiety can be overwhelming, it is like a wave: initially strong, but the longer you stay with it, the weaker it gets. Avoidance is what makes anxiety strong, and surfing anxiety means you aren't running from it. Often it's the initial surge of anxiety that scares a child and makes them want to avoid places like school and birthday parties, and experiences like patting animals and riding a bike for the first time. Generally once a child has faced the initial anxiety of a new situation and surfed it out, their confidence will be stronger and they'll be more inclined to face the situation again.

Together with your child, start surfing your emotional discomfort in a variety of situations so you can rate it. It's only when your child can measure their own anxiety that they can do something to reduce it. The situations you choose for this should be mildly anxiety-provoking, in the form of a challenge, but still fun. Types of practice situations include:

* having a cold shower
* holding an ice cube in your hand (make sure it is a bit wet to avoid freezer burn)

* eating ice-cream quickly to bring on a mild and temporary headache (better suited to older children)

* drinking a fizzy drink quickly so that it makes your eyes water

* standing in a squatting position against the wall, like you're sitting in an imaginary chair, so that your leg muscles work to hold you in this pose (If you or your child have an injury or physical complaint, check with your physician first before doing this exercise).

The third and final ingredient for helping your child face a fear is making a game out of it. Children learn best when playing. By making a game out of facing minor fears, you are getting past your child's defences and cleverly laying down the neural blueprint in their brain for managing larger fears.

Please note, by 'fear-provoking situation' I do not mean anything dangerous that will place you or your child's physical or psychological wellbeing in jeopardy. I'm referring to small, everyday fears your child would easily conquer. Using yourself as a model, have a competition with your child where you both have to do something small that scares you. Examples of mild fears you could both make a game out of include:

Parent fears	Child fears
Skip for a short way in public.	Pop a balloon with a pin.
Beep the car horn for no reason.	Get something out of your room on your own at night time.
Wear something you wouldn't normally wear.	Ask and pay for your own ice-cream at a shop.
Pick up a small harmless spider (such as a daddy-long-legs) in the house and move it outside.	Handle something smelly while wearing gloves, such as picking up dog poo, a dead animal or insect and putting it in the bin, or turning the compost.

If your child is initially reluctant to play the game, try playing for a reward of some description. The reward may be a treat, being allowed to stay up after their bedtime or going to see a movie. Base this on your own child's motivations as many children will find that simple praise from you, combined with seeing you step out of a comfort zone, is reward enough. Remember, regardless of what the reward is, make the game fun without being too competitive, as it's non-serious fun that provides the best environment for learning.

Summing up

We all feel fear, but those who can manage it have a distinct advantage over those who can't. Teach your child to break down facing a fear into small, manageable steps. While stepping out of their comfort zone, have them rate their discomfort so that they can see that when they surf their fear it drops like a wave. And finally, make a game out of fear. The more enjoyable, the more you will be helping to lay the neural foundation in your child's brain for managing fear. Starting today, what small comfort zone can you model stepping out of to your child?

4

LET THEM SEE THE DEAD GOLDFISH

'Healthy children will not fear life if their elders have integrity enough not to fear death.'

ERIK H. ERIKSON

Even though death is a natural part of life, most people in society are terrified of it. For parents, this can be especially true if it's the death of a child's pet.

As Samantha walked back into the house after dropping her young son, Alex, at school, she looked up and saw it. There in front of her was Alex's pet goldfish, Flash, upside down in its tank. Samantha was instantly overcome with the sickening feeling of how Alex would react to Flash's death.

She quickly got on the phone to her husband, Mike. Upon hearing his distraught wife, Mike knew what needed to be done. They had to find a replacement goldfish before Alex came home from school. Mike left work early and raced down to the pet shop. There were some fish very similar in size and colour to Flash, but none were identical. He phoned his wife, and they both agreed that Alex probably wouldn't even notice the difference. The new fish was bought.

When Alex got home, his parents hid their anxiety by trying to act like nothing had happened. Alex took one look at them and asked if anything was wrong. Both parents simultaneously replied with an emphatic no. About half an hour later, Alex was walking past his fish tank. Upon seeing the fish he screamed, 'Cool, a new fish, but where's Flash?' Mike and Samantha looked at each other blankly for support. Samantha opened her arms to cuddle her son. Mike cleared his throat and then explained to Alex that Flash had died and gone to heaven. Alex was quiet for a moment, and then in an excited voice asked, 'Where did you put his body?' The fish was retrieved from the bin, followed by a small ceremony and burial in the backyard.

If you are like Mike and Samantha, and are worried about discussing death with your child, you're not alone. By trying to hide the dead pet, Alex's parents believed they were protecting Alex emotionally. When we avoid talking about something that is obviously upsetting, such as the death of a pet, children like Alex are given the message that if Mum and Dad can't talk about it, it really must be bad so they'd better not talk about it either. The problem is that instead of protecting a child by avoiding talking about death, we risk making the child more worried and keep them from telling us how they feel.

Leaving a child to fill in the blanks about death can be disastrous as they don't yet have the brain development to understand the world as an adult can. As a result children will come up with amazing explanations for death, such as:

* Death is punishment for bad behaviour.

* Death is a person or monster who takes you away.

* Death is somehow contagious.

* If you walk on a grave the deceased person feels it.

* If Grandma has gone to live in the sky and continues to eat and drink and play cards with her friends up there, then I must be the reason she doesn't come back to visit.

Even when we don't talk about something we are still communicating. Children are great observers and as parents we are constantly communicating messages to them by what we do, say and don't say. Whether it's the tone of your voice or your body language, children are constantly reading the cues their parents give. This all happens whether a parent is aware of it or not, and is all the more important to realise when difficult topics such as death arise.

Talk to your child

Talking to your child about death will allow you to discover what they do and don't know about the topic, as well as any misconceptions or fears they may have. If there are any mistaken beliefs your child holds about death, you can help correct them by providing information, comfort and understanding.

How you talk about death with your child, and the right time to discuss it, will depend on their age and experience with the topic. If your child has never been directly affected by death, you will have to approach it differently. It will also depend on your own experiences, religious beliefs, feelings and the situation at the time. Discussions about death may be prompted by a news report, television program or seeing a dead animal beside the road. These talks are often good as they can take place in a relatively unemotional atmosphere. However, discussions may result from a family crisis or the death of a friend's family member, which are likely to be charged with emotions. It's best if you can start talking about death before a crisis occurs. This way you will be able to discuss the topic when emotions are calm.

How to talk about death with your child

TALK SIMPLY Communicating with a young child about death can be challenging because they need short and simple explanations. Long, complicated responses to their questions will only bore or confuse them. Instead, use short, concrete examples they understand, such as explaining what the dead person or animal can no longer do. For example, when people die they do not breathe, eat, talk, think or feel anymore; when fish die they do not swim or blow bubbles anymore; dead flowers do not grow or blossom anymore.

BE HONEST If your child asks a question about death that you don't know the answer to, say so. An honest 'I just don't know the answer to that one' is often more comforting than an explanation that the parent doesn't quite believe themselves. Why? Your child will often sense your discomfort, and it's this discomfort that activates a child's danger alarm. An honest 'I just don't know' will do more good than a well-intentioned lie.

READ A SUITABLE BOOK TOGETHER It can be useful to get an appropriate children's book on the topic and read it with your child. Ask your local library or bookshop for titles most suited to your child's age, as children will cope with death differently depending on their developmental stage in life.

PLAY GAMES INCORPORATING DEATH Children learn best through games. Join in with your child and play dolls, cars, drawing or whatever they enjoy. As you are playing, ask what would happen if the doll, toy or car died. Be prepared to correct any faulty beliefs your child may have about death. Often it can be of benefit to incorporate a make-believe funeral in the game as this can help further uncover faulty beliefs. If your child doesn't take to playing games of this nature, ask them to draw where your pet would go if it died.

Summing up

No matter how children cope with death, or express their feelings, they need sympathetic and non-judgemental responses from adults. Encourage your child to talk about death, whether through open talking, reading a suitable book together or incorporating death in a child's game or art. If you can permit your child to talk to you about death, you can better prepare them if and when they are upset. Remember, you can make it easier for your child to talk if you are open, honest and comfortable with your own feelings about death. It takes courage to talk about death with your child. Yet doing so will pay dividends in helping foster your child's confidence.

5

LET YOUR CHILD STRUGGLE

*'The hardest part of raising a child
is teaching them to ride bicycles. A
shaky child on a bicycle for the first
time needs both support and freedom.
The realization that this is what the
child will always need can hit hard.'*

SLOAN WILSON

Watching the awkwardness of a child trying to use a paint
brush, put on their clothes, do up buttons, hit a nail with
a hammer, brush their hair or tie a knot can be extremely
frustrating. Often parents will naturally want to intervene
and do the task for their child. Doing so can be potentially

limiting in helping a child develop 'mastery motivation', a term psychologists use to describe a person's ability to stick at a task until it is mastered.

I saw Erica for counselling as she was feeling extremely stressed by her mother's interference in her wedding preparations. This was nothing new: her mother had jumped in and done everything for her since childhood. Erica recalled that when she was eight, she carefully cut a tomato to help her rushed mother prepare tea. Upon seeing Erica's finished work, her mother gruffly said, 'I could have done it quicker.' Whether it was sewing, cooking, spelling, homework, jigsaw puzzles, painting or making any kind of decision, her mother always stepped in when Erica appeared to be struggling. This taught Erica that she was incompetent. Now, with the wedding fast approaching and her mother trying to do everything so Erica wouldn't struggle, Erica needed to be assertive and make the tough decisions herself. But she had never done anything by herself without her mother intervening.

It's a natural urge for parents to want to step in and support a child they think is struggling. However, there's a fine line between supporting and rescuing, especially once your child grows up. Rescuing teaches the child that they are incompetent and can't be trusted. Supporting, on the other hand, allows your child to try new challenges without your direct intervention. If rescuing is always running along and holding on to the back of your child's bike as they learn to ride, supporting is letting go when the child is ready and being prepared for the child to fall. The supporting approach may seem harsh – *let* your child fall off the bike? But even with all its risks the 'supporting approach' is more beneficial. Why is this? The problem with rescuing a child when they are struggling with a new task is that it robs them of practical experience. It's this practical experience that develops both new neural connections in the brain and the 'mastery motivation' of sticking to a new task until it is mastered.

When a child embarks on a new task, no matter how awkward they seem, they are creating new neural pathways in their brain – the key to learning any new skill or talent – and developing mastery motivation. Initially a child will seem clumsy but the more they repeat a task, the stronger the neural connections in the brain for that particular task. Imagine that creating new neural connections in the brain is like skiing down a mountain that hasn't been skied before. Initially you will be cautious and go very slowly, looking out for hidden dangers under the snow. The next time you'll be able to follow your initial ski tracks, allowing you to be that little bit more confident. Each time you go down the mountain following the same tracks, these tracks become more worn, allowing you to go faster and faster. The same occurs with neural connections in the brain: the more you repeat a new task, the more worn the neural pathways in the brain become. Repetition is the key to mastering any new task.

Learning through repetition comes naturally to children. They unconsciously know that mastering any new task requires repetition. However, as adults we seem to lose sight of this vital ingredient for success. As a result, many adults will only try something new once. If the adult fails to master the task on the first go, their motivation to try again is gone and they reason that they are no good at that particular task. Allow your child to be a child and to keep trying to master a task, no matter how much they struggle. If a child doesn't want to do something, they will let you know. Just make sure you aren't the one to plant the seed in their mind that they can't do it, robbing them of the motivation to continue.

How can you help your child develop mastery motivation? The golden rule is to *pause* that little bit longer before giving your child help. Here is a short list of potential ways to help your child develop mastery motivation, which may give you ideas for other areas:

* Count to five before telling your child the correct pronunciation of the word they are having trouble reading.

* Have your child cut a difficult shape out of paper with scissors.

* Have your child write their name or catch a tennis ball with their non-dominant hand.

* If you are checking their homework, before telling them what the mistakes are, point to their incorrect answer and see if they can work out for themselves where the mistake is and what the correct answer should be.

* Let them help you cook something in the kitchen, and don't intervene with their set tasks unless they ask for help. *Note:* If your child's safety is being threatened by flames, knives or electricity, then you should of course intervene.

With any of these tasks it's important to pause before helping your child. Generally if they really need help they will ask. However, if your child is inclined to always ask for help without even really trying themselves, your aim is to help build self-efficacy or confidence in their own ability. Do this by first simplifying the task, for example, catching the ball with both hands instead of just one. Then show that you believe in your child's ability to complete the task by being encouraging, supportive and patient. When a child understands that their parent believes in their ability to complete a task, the child becomes motivated to prove their parent right.

Summing up

By standing back and watching your child struggle with everyday situations that aren't threatening or dangerous, you are inadvertently teaching them mastery motivation and developing their brain. Be encouraging of your child's efforts, and be slow to do things for them that they could do themselves. What is something physically awkward you can encourage your child to do?

6

TAKE TIME TO SMELL THE ROSES

'The ability to be in the present moment is a major component of mental wellness.'

ABRAHAM MASLOW

The secret of happiness is not doing what one likes, but liking what one has to do. This is achieved by deliberately focusing your mind in the present moment, a psychological technique called mindfulness. Thanks to modern science, brain scans have shown that when a person is thinking in the present moment, it's impossible to feel anxiety or depression. Psychologists are not sure why this is, but they have basically determined that anxiety occurs when the mind is thinking about the future and depression occurs when thinking about the past. Yet when the mind can be focused on right now, a natural calmness is experienced.

Tracy was a worrywart who would go at full pace the whole time, like a mini-tornado. She'd worry excessively about her children's safety and wellbeing, as well as all the jobs she hadn't done. Her sleep was often broken as she woke from worry, fearing that the oven had been left on, that their home insurance wasn't up to date or that the school cake day was the next day. Even when Tracy was playing with her children at the park, her mind couldn't focus on what they were doing because she'd be alert to all the potential risks associated with the park. Whenever she paused long enough to reflect on her life, she'd feel down, thinking of how the worry had stopped her from leading a happy life.

Even though Tracy's is excessive, worry is a common part of parenting. As a parent, I'm often thinking about the potential worst-case scenario. So why do we worry? The human brain, unlike any other animal brain on the planet, is unique for one very special trick that it can perform. It is able to predict the timing and location of dangers before they actually happen. In other words, we are able to dodge something that isn't coming at us yet. Without this response to potential threats, we wouldn't have dental floss, car seatbelts, vaccinations, superannuation or insurance.

Future thinking for parents can be both a blessing, in helping keep our children safe, and a curse, in stressing us out and prompting us to wrap our children in cotton wool.

Even though we can't always live with our minds in the present moment, we can certainly increase the amount of time we do sit in the present. For most of us, our minds rarely, if ever, go there. How do you get your mind to stay in the present for short periods of time? The key is to focus on at least one of your five senses – sight, sound, smell, touch or taste – while engaging in something. Do this by simply noticing how your senses respond to a specific object or situation, but without passing judgement as to whether the experience is good, bad or indifferent. The moment you pass judgement while trying to focus on your senses, your mind has to go either into the past or the future so it can make a comparison and form an opinion. When this happens you'll be cut off from your five senses as well as the present moment.

Teach your child mindfulness by doing the following exercises with them. Make sure you keep the exercises fun as this allows the mind to more easily stay in the present moment:

* **TOUCH** Notice and describe how it feels to pat the family pet or walk on soft grass/sand/in water without wearing shoes. Or, when walking, simply

notice your feet – is your big toe the first to touch or leave the ground? Does your foot roll from side to side? Does your foot land toe- or heel-first?

* **SMELL** Smell a rose, flower or leaf and notice its scent and how the scent feels as it enters your nostrils.

* **SOUND** Close your eyes for thirty seconds and notice all the different sounds around you. Then at the end of the thirty seconds repeat back as many things as you can remember hearing. Children love this game.

* **TASTE** Eat different foods blindfolded and try to guess what they are. Make sure you describe the tastes in detail – sweet, salty, sour, rough or smooth instead of just yucky or yummy.

* **SIGHT** For thirty seconds try to memorise all the different things around you. Then at the end of the thirty seconds, close your eyes and repeat back as many things as you can remember seeing.

When doing these activities with your child, you may need to go first to demonstrate to your child what you notice with your senses. This way you will be modelling how the game works and what is required of them.

What if my mind wanders?

While playing with your child, it's normal and okay for your mind to wander and think about all the things you should be doing, such as work. Remember, the mind is constantly thinking and will naturally head in the future or the past looking for a task to focus on. Gently bring your mind back to the present moment by focusing on one or more of your senses. The rule is to be kind to yourself when your mind does wander.

Summing up

Encouraging your child to spend time in the present moment is a great way of combating stress, theirs as well as yours. Do this by teaching your child to get in touch with their five senses in response to the environment around them. Not only does mindfulness act as a form of time out for the mind, but it also allows a person to concentrate better on the task at hand. Take your child and go smell the roses.

7

CONQUERING FEAR IS ABOUT PATIENCE

'A habit cannot be tossed out the window; it must be coaxed down the stairs a step at a time.'

MARK TWAIN

We all feel fear. It is there to protect us from danger. Yet many adults believe that fear is harmful and, if their child feels it, it's a sign of weakness. Toby said that he didn't want to give a speech in class because he was scared. His parents told him, 'You'll be fine!' and changed the subject to try to keep his mind off it. Many parents believe the best way to help their child to not be fearful is to keep their mind on something else. Even though the distraction technique has its place in certain specific situations, such as getting an injection, for other areas, like giving a speech, it can risk making the child feel both unheard and weak for feeling fear.

Research shows that people who don't feel fear are at risk of hurting themselves because they can't identify dangerous situations. It's like a child who runs out on the road to retrieve a ball, but doesn't perceive the travelling cars as a threat. Usually a person who is genuinely fearless, as opposed to one who is lying about being fearless, is that way because of brain damage. Certain stroke victims, where the part of the brain that modulates fear has been damaged by the stroke, have been shown frightening video footage from horror movies and real-life documentaries. Because their brains can't interpret signals of fear, they show no sign of distress and often become bored watching things that would give you and me nightmares.

So resist unrealistic expectations that your child should be fearless. Courage comes from feeling fear while still continuing to move towards a chosen goal, such as speaking in class, talking to someone new or staying overnight at a friend's house. If it's normal to feel fear when trying something new, how can you help your child manage their fear?

Fear is potentially the most misunderstood emotion. Adults often think that the only way to handle fear is to face it head-on – throwing a young child in the deep end of the pool to help beat their fear of water, for instance. Facing a fear head-on can work, but it is a huge gamble. It has the potential to go horribly wrong and make the fear stronger and lower one's self-confidence, especially in children. Once a child's self-confidence has been lost in a certain area, it can be very difficult to get it back.

How can you help your child face a fearful situation and build their confidence? First of all, listen to your child talk about their fear and let them know that it's normal to feel the way they do. You could tell them that you felt the same way when you were a child. Your aim is to reassure your child that they will be fine. Secondly, building on chapter 3, help your child face their fear in small, realistic steps. This is something athletes and even racehorses do all the time. They build up to a main event over a long period of time by competing in plenty of smaller events first. A racehorse owner will first race the horse in a small event out in the country, then progress to a slightly larger race with more horses and spectators. The difficulty of each race will progressively increase until eventually the horse is racing the Melbourne Cup. This is achievable because the final goal of racing in the Melbourne Cup was first broken down into steps.

Like a racehorse, you need to help your child break down fearful situations into manageable steps. A word of caution, these steps need to be child-sized, not adult ones. Let your child control the tempo. Using the example of facing the fear of water, let's break it down and show how to help a child take swimming lessons. Remember, this formula can be applied to *any* situation.

Possible steps for facing the fear of water:

* **STEP 1:** Take your child to visit the local pool without going in the water.

* **STEP 2:** On the next visit, sit by the edge of the pool and have your child put their feet in the water.

* **STEP 3:** Next visit, sit by the edge of the pool and pour a cup of water over their legs or lower body.

* **STEP 4:** Let your child walk into the pool up to their knees (if the pool's depth will allow this).

* **STEP 5:** Hold your child's hand and gradually walk into the pool up to their waist.

The time taken to do these steps will be determined by your child. It might be done quickly, with more than one step completed at each visit, or over a few weeks, depending on your child. Let them be the boss. Remember, each time they take a step forward, reward them with praise and maybe even a treat. Rewarded behaviour gets repeated.

Summing up

We all feel fear. However, what may be nothing to an adult can be absolutely terrifying to a child. Therefore, respect your child's fear by listening to and acknowledging their worries instead of dismissing them. Break down facing the fear into small manageable steps. Be patient and take the time to help your child. Confidence is fragile; treat it with care. Your goal is to build your child's confidence, and this takes time.

8

PAUSE BEFORE PUNISHING

'The right word may be effective, but no word was ever as effective as a rightly timed pause.'

MARK TWAIN

Read the sign below and see if you notice anything.

How did you go? You may not have noticed that the word 'the' appears twice. If you already know the illusion, try it on someone who doesn't. The illusion works because we fall into the trap of only focusing on certain parts of the statement, usually the descriptive words like 'bird' and 'bush', while overlooking the more common word 'the'. This leads a person to assume they know what they are looking at without taking in the whole situation properly. In a similar way, when it comes to disciplining a child, parents can make bad judgements in the heat of the moment by seeing only what they think are the important parts of the story. This can lead to cruel and hurtful comments, as well as a child being punished more harshly than they deserve.

Ian was punished harshly in public by his father after he pushed another boy over and made him cry. Even though Ian's approach may not have been the best option, if his father had asked Ian to explain his actions before yelling and hitting him in public, he would have found out that the boy had actually been teasing Ian's little sister and had pushed her over.

Like the illusion above, Ian's father made a judgement without looking at the whole situation first. The key to not falling into this trap when punishing your child is to look at each individual item before trying to interpret the situation. The simple way to achieve this is to pause before punishing your child. Take three deep breaths and study the situation. Have you taken in all the information or is there something you have missed? It only takes an extra ten seconds, but pausing will give your mind time to take in the whole situation, look at things more rationally and prevent you from jumping to conclusions.

Thankfully my own father paused before punishing me in my childhood, when I nearly burned the family home down. I was about ten years old and had made a secret hideout under the house, equipped with its own fireplace, a leftover empty paint tin. I placed some paper in the tin and lit it to make the hideout complete. But the dried paint in the tin was highly flammable and flames quickly shot up and started licking the underside of the house's floorboards. In a panic, I tried to pick the tin up and race it out from under the house but, because it was so hot, it burned my hands. I ran inside, white with fear, and screamed to Mum and Dad that the house was going to burn down. My father rushed under the house and successfully put the fire out.

Once our heart rates returned to normal, I knew I was going to be in serious trouble. Even though I hadn't intentionally tried to burn the house down, I knew my act of negligence wouldn't go unpunished. My father looked at me, ready to dish out my punishment, and noticed I was clutching my badly burnt and blistered hands. All the adrenalin had made me lose sight of how painful and badly burnt they were. I remember the look in my father's eyes as he paused and studied my hands. It was only a short pause, but it felt like an eternity. A calm came over his face like a decision had been made. He said that my burnt hands were punishment enough and he helped me put them under cold running water. He wasn't wrong – for quite some time burnt hands stopped me from riding my bike, playing sport, writing, playing on the computer and anything else that required my hands. I was effectively grounded without being grounded and there was no one I could blame.

Summing up

Like in the illusion at the start of the chapter, it's simple to overlook important points that we may have taken for granted. Before dealing out a decision, punishment or your opinion to your child, pause. Take three deep breaths and look twice at a situation to make sure you have taken in everything. Courage can be fostered by providing an environment where a child can make accurate predictions about how you'll respond to a situation based on how you have responded in the past. The more calmly you respond, the more inclined they will be to try new things and share these experiences with you. Achieve this by simply pausing before punishing.

9

CRY FOR YOUR CHILD'S HEALTH

'Tears are the safety valve of the heart when too much pressure is laid on it.'

ALBERT SMITH

Humans are the only primates that cry. Only one other land animal cries – the elephant. Crying is a vital factor in health maintenance as it releases emotions and stress. It comes naturally to young children, and adults could learn from their example. Research shows that crying benefits health in three ways: 1) decreasing negative emotions such as depression; 2) releasing stress-related biochemical toxins (tears shed while watching a sad movie are shown to have more protein than tears shed due to cutting an onion); and 3) decreasing the nervous system's response to stress.

With the benefits that come from crying, experts suggest that because men cry less than women they suffer more stress-related diseases and die younger. What's more, people who are reluctant to cry are also more inclined not to ask for help when they need it most. Often the more fearless and 'emotionally hardened' a person is, the more terrified they are of expressing their emotions. Not wanting to cry stems largely from a perceived stigma of appearing weak or vulnerable if emotions are expressed.

A father came to me for counselling after his wife was tragically killed in a car accident, leaving him to raise three young children by himself. But he didn't come to counselling for himself. He came because he was worried about his teenage son. He hadn't cried at his mother's funeral, refused to talk about her and was bottling up his emotions. As the father described his son's problem of bottling up emotions, I asked him how he himself was coping. He looked at me sternly and said that he didn't have time to grieve because he was too busy looking after everyone else. It turned out that the boy was merely emulating his father's emotional response to grief. I pointed out that the father was role modelling to his son how to deal with emotions – bottle them up. Upon hearing this, he froze and then burst into tears.

Later in the session he told me that he was absolutely terrified of crying. His reasoning was that if he started

10

MAKE TIME TO WASTE TIME

*'Cleaning your house while your kids
are still growing up is like shoveling
the walk before it stops snowing.'*

PHYLLIS DILLER

Psychologists have discovered that play is vital for a child's
development as it helps foster motivation, control, a sense
of reality, imagination and cognitive ability and even helps
reduce stress. Most parents acknowledge how important
play is for children; though most parents, if they were
honest, would admit that they'd prefer their child to play
without them. When it comes to playing with their child,
many parents feel that there are other jobs that need to
be done and they don't have the time. This only sets off

a parent's inbuilt guilt meter that they are neglecting their child.

Shelley was a good mum who often felt guilty that she wasn't the perfect parent for her daughter, Lily. Even though Shelley attended to Lily's physical and emotional needs, when it came time to playing with her, Lily could point out the exact moment that her mum's mind started wandering. This was usually when Shelley spotted the basket of folded clothes that needed to be put away.

In contrast, Lily's dad, Roger, took playing far more seriously. Due to Roger's busy work schedule, he had limited time that he could commit to Lily. To make up for his guilt for not spending time with his daughter, Roger made sure that whenever he played with Lily the play provided her with a definite learning goal, such as teaching Lily how to make a structurally sound cubbyhouse out of cushions, get the best possible score at putt-putt golf, or paint a picture that included letters to improve Lily's word comprehension. But Roger was really making the playtime more stimulating for himself – playing dolls and dress-ups seemed like a bad use of time. Even though Shelley's and Roger's views on playing differed, they shared the same view towards time – they didn't have enough to enjoy with their daughter.

Can you relate to these time-poor play sessions? Do you become agitated thinking of all the other things you should be doing when you're playing with your child? Or do you deliberately try to structure playtime to prevent yourself becoming bored? Whatever your approach, it's likely that you'll have three problems to deal with: 1) limited time to play with your child; 2) feelings of boredom while playing with your child; and 3) feelings of guilt sparked by the previous two points. Let's have a look at ways you can deal with these three issues so that you can increase your enjoyment when playing with your child.

Make time to waste time

Since researchers discovered the physical and psychological benefits of a child playing, pressure has been placed on parents to be the 'perfect parent': to be more structured and to choose the perfect activity for their child's playtime. It would be interesting to know what impact the 'perfect parenting' ethos has had on the guilt levels of today's time-poor parents. After all, most parents today could safely say that their own parents didn't spend the same amount of time playing with them as they are expected to spend with their child now. Here is the problem: parents are expected to spend more time playing with their children than any generation before them but have more commitments and less time than any generation before them. What is the answer?

Parents need to take time management to a whole new level and actually waste time instead of trying to save it.

If the thought of wasting 'precious' time makes you anxious and uncomfortable, you could try wasting time deliberately. Using a bit of reverse psychology and allowing yourself to waste time helps put on hold the high expectations you have for yourself, so you can enjoy the time with your child. The rule here is to set aside a realistic amount of time to waste and stick to it. Often parents feel overwhelmed thinking that they'll have to play with their child for hours on end. If time is an issue, start off with setting aside ten minutes every second day to waste. Start small so you can get used to wasting time. If your blood pressure has risen just at the thought of wasting time deliberately, you're very normal. Let's have a look at how this can be done to best benefit both you and your child.

Play in the present

As discussed in the previous chapter, when the mind is in the present moment it's impossible to feel anxiety or depression, or any emotions related to them, such as boredom, guilt and stress. Generally parents will fall victim to 'future thinking' when playing with their child, thinking about all the things they should be doing instead of playing. A great way to get your mind in the present is to approach play as a child does, and make it fun and non-serious. The more fun you have, the easier it is for your mind to forget the outcome of the game and instead stay in the present moment.

What is play? Play can best be defined as a state of mind rather than the specific characteristics of the activity itself. Play is focused more on the process, of just having fun, rather than being outcome-focused – it's still effective even if only half of the jigsaw puzzle is put back together. Probably the most important criterion that makes play effective is that it's non-serious.

How can you help make play non-serious? One simple factor that defines play as being too serious, as opposed to non-serious and fun, is that serious play is generally cleaner. The messier a game is (within reason), the less serious and the more engaging it will be, meaning your mind will be less likely to wander. It's a lot harder for a child to get dirty or make a mess when they're playing academically stimulating games than when they're playing for the fun of it, like jumping in puddles.

Examples of messy activities that are non-serious and fun:

*   playing in the rain
*   splashing in puddles
*   making mud cakes and getting dirty
*   hand painting
*   playing at the park with your child (with you on the swings too)

* making a cave under the bed covers and hiding

* cooking in the kitchen.

I'm not saying that every time you play with your child it should be messy. This would be totally unrealistic and you'd be forever soaking their clothes for stains. But make sure that at some point during the week/fortnight/month you incorporate at least one messy play activity with your child. Not only will your child love it, but you'll be more inclined to feel like you can waste time without the guilt.

Summing up

Play is a very important part of a healthy child's development. By allowing yourself to waste time with your child you'll help deal with feelings of guilt. Practise keeping your mind focused on the present moment when you play with your child by making the activity non-serious, fun, process-focused instead of outcome-focused and, where possible, messy. Go on, waste time with your child; find a puddle, jump in it and get dirty.

11

PUT *YOU* BEFORE YOUR CHILD

'The name of the game is taking care of yourself, because you're going to live long enough to wish you had.'

GRACE MIRABELLA

If you have ever been on a plane you'll be familiar with the supposedly reassuring safety demonstration in the event of an emergency, which is done right at the start of the flight. The flight attendants demonstrate how to put the oxygen mask over the face, and special attention is given to parents travelling with children. Parents are instructed to put themselves first in the event of an emergency, placing the oxygen mask over their own face before their child's. This is because a parent's natural instinct is to look after their child first, making the parent more susceptible to passing out from lack of oxygen. Once the parent passes out, both the child and parent are in danger, so it's vital that parents resist the urge and put themselves before their child. This is vital not only for surviving plane disasters but also for raising a happy and confident child.

The psychologist Carl Jung once said, 'Show me a sane man and I will cure him for you.' Building on this I would say, 'Show me a stress-free parent and I will cure them for you.' Most of us can't afford full-time nannies to raise our children. Therefore we are vulnerable to suffering from stress caused by parenting. The danger with this is that you can inadvertently pass on your stress to your child. It's crucial for both you and your family that you take time to look after yourself. How can you do this?

Have a mini-moon

A honeymoon is designed to be a time where a couple can have a break from the stressors of the world and focus on their new life together. In a similar way, it is important that a parent is able to have a short break from the daily stress of parenting. If a top racehorse is expected to win, it must be rested after each race. Yet as parents we race every day with little or no breaks and expect to somehow just keep winning. You can only do this for so long until your stress starts affecting the family. For the sake of your child and yourself, take a mini-moon. Ways you can have a mini-moon:

* Get a babysitter so you can have an afternoon, evening or night off and feel human again.

* Make time to sit and have a cuppa.

* Take up an interest that is realistically achievable, e.g. some form of art.

* Catch up with friends.

* Get a massage (think of the cost as an investment in your family's happiness) or have a bubble bath.

If you are having trouble working out what to do, sometimes asking yourself the following question can help: 'What were you doing the last time you laughed a lot?'

Remember, your mini-moon doesn't have to be anything over the top or unrealistic. If an overseas holiday without children isn't doable, find something that you can realistically achieve.

Be prepared to feel guilt

Sally decided that she was going to make time for herself. She waited until she had the house to herself and made herself a cuppa, sat down and started to read her book. However, it wasn't long before an inner voice started saying that Sally was being selfish. She lifted her eyes from the page and saw the basket of clothes that needed folding and putting away. Guilt started to set in. Then she realised that she really should start preparing a 'proper' dinner instead of the quick and easy meal she had planned. The more Sally thought about all the things she should be doing, the more the guilt flooded in, until eventually she put the book down and resigned herself to her chores.

Can you relate to Sally's experience? The biggest barrier parents find when trying to have time to themselves is guilt. This could be the guilt of not doing work (from housework to paid work) or of having a short break away from the family, even if it's locking yourself away in the bathroom to have a bubble bath. The trick in dealing with guilt is to expect it to come and then ride it out when it does. Guilt will initially be strong, but if you can resist the urge to put others first, this guilt will soon drop, and drop quickly. A great way to deal with the guilt is to keep reminding yourself that you are having time off for the sake of your family. Happy parents have happy children.

Summing up

Having a short break from the usual grind will help rest you. When a person is rested they are in a far better position psychologically to deal with the stressors of life, especially parenting. This way you'll be less likely to pass on your stress to your child. Remember, a rested parent is a happy parent, something children love.

12

WALK YOUR TALK

'While your children may appear to not
be listening to you, you can be sure
they'll be faithful in imitating you.'

ANONYMOUS

Children are influenced more by their parents' actions than their words. How often have you seen or heard your child do or say something that you do? Your child is watching, copying and learning from your actions.

Sandra was a vegetarian and very health-conscious. She gave her son, James, only vegetarian food and avoided processed food because she wanted to give him the best start in life. But Sandra loved eating her favourite burger, without the meat, from a well-known fast food chain. She would take James into the restaurant and they would both have lunch together. Sandra would eat her meatless burger while James would have to eat the sandwiches she had packed for him. One day, James looked at his mum eating her burger and asked, 'Why am I not allowed to eat food here, but you are?'

Even though this seems to be a relatively harmless example of giving a child mixed messages, we are all guilty of falling into a similar trap as parents. Sometimes we don't want to face up to our double standards, because if we do we might realise we need to change, and this change can be uncomfortable. How often have you heard another parent say to their child, 'Do as I say, not as I do'? Unfortunately, children don't hear a parent's words as loudly as they hear their parent's actions. Research shows that children are constantly watching and imitating their parents, even in the most subtle of ways.

Whether parents like it or not, their actions provide the framework for their child for how to handle their own personal issues. I'm not trying to put the fear of god into every parent who reads this; my aim is not for you to be paranoid about your every action. Instead, my intention is for you to be aware of what your actions are saying. Once you become aware of this, you can match your words to your actions so as to avoid the trap of giving mixed messages to your child.

There are two common mixed-message traps parents fall into with their child:

1. Making promises you can't fill.

2. Having two sets of rules: one for the parent and one for the child, e.g. the parent who smokes, but doesn't want their child to.

Let's take a look at each of these traps individually.

Trap 1: Making promises you can't fill

An old saying goes, 'There's no such thing as perfect people, only perfect intentions.' If you have had someone promise you something but their perfect intentions never transformed into action, you know how crushing it can be. Children have excellent memories for unkept promises.

Craig's father always promised that he would build him a tree house. When Craig asked about the tree house, his father had him draw plans of how he wanted it to be. Time passed and still no tree house. Whenever Craig asked about it, his father would apologise by explaining that work was very busy at the moment. As a nine-year-old, Craig was confused because his father said he was busy but would then sit down and watch TV or go and play golf with friends on the weekend.

Before you promise your child anything, ask yourself, 'Am I prepared to follow through on this promise?' If the answer is no, don't make the promise. A child's confidence is fragile, and broken promises by adults will only serve to lower it. Yes, there will come times in your child's life where other people will not follow up on their promises. However, as a parent, by keeping your promises you are teaching your child that a promise is a commitment.

Trap 2: Having two sets of rules

Having two sets of rules in your home, one for your child and another for yourself, is a sure way of giving off mixed messages and confusing your child. Common ways parents fall into the 'two sets of rules' trap are:

* The parents who push their child to master a musical instrument, but are unable to play any instrument themselves.

* The father who criticises his son's fitness levels at a local sporting match, but is overweight and never exercises himself.

* The parent who tells their child not to take up smoking and drinking like they have because it's bad for their health.

* The parent who threatens to punish their child if they ever try to watch any of their parents' horror movies.

* The mother who refuses to share her make-up with her young daughter, explaining that true beauty is on the inside.

Where possible, ensure that you have only one set of rules in your home. Lead by example: if it's good enough for your child to do with or without something, then it's good enough for you. For example, if you want your child to learn a musical instrument, learn one yourself. If your child's fitness levels aren't where they should be, then first focus on getting your own fitness levels right. When a child sees their parent try something new, struggle, but persevere, it normalises stepping out of comfort zones and empowers the child to do the same. This is a potent way of developing a child's self-efficacy.

The lessons learned in childhood will give a person a strong foundation to act from in later life. For example, if you model healthy eating habits to your child as they are growing up, when they are old enough to make their own decisions they might at times choose to drink excessively and eat poorly. But when they are feeling really grotty there is more chance that they will go back to the healthy eating you have taught them through your example.

Summing up

Your child will naturally copy your actions. Parents who aren't aware of this risk falling into the trap of giving mixed messages. Capitalise on your child's natural copycat tendencies. If you want to increase the chance of your child being interested in science, read science books yourself; if

13

PLAY 'FOLLOW THE LEADER'

'Life is like a dogsled team: unless you're the lead dog, the scenery never changes.'

LEWIS GRIZZARD

Leadership skills are very important for a child to have. However, their ability to lead themselves when around other people is even more important. This is because humans are naturally herd animals, and the herd's influence often unknowingly affects the choices we make. Researchers are now claiming that humans' brains have evolved to such a sophisticated level that we are capable of estimating and handling potential threats like no other animal on earth. Instead of reacting instinctively to danger through the fight-or-flight response, humans are able to stay in a scary situation while being able to analyse it more accurately and determine options for handling it. This ability to estimate threat has developed not because of environmental demands but because of social demands. We have developed a social brain, hardwired for helping us get along with the greatest threat to humans: other people.

At four or five, children start to develop social cognition, the ability to interpret the actions of themselves and others. This is a vital skill as humans are group animals, instinctively needing other people. Psychologists have found that when a person is ostracised from a group, it actually dulls the brain and decreases the ability for intelligent thought. When a person feels accepted into a group, their ability to think is much better.

How many people do you have in your general circle of friends? Psychologist Professor Dunbar from Oxford University has shown that, for most of us, the number is approximately 150. This is because 150 is about the maximum number of meaningful relationships (where both people know a lot about each other, e.g. family, friends, close neighbours, work colleagues, team mates) that the adult human brain can handle. Interestingly, Professor Dunbar observed that within this group of 150 people the average person will have approximately:

* five intimate friends (support)

* fifteen close friends (sympathy)

* fifty reasonably close friends, such as family and neighbours

* eighty people who are less close but still in a person's social group.

Professor Dunbar's findings highlight the fact that we potentially have a lot more people involved in our lives than we may think. And even if you don't have 150 people in your circle of friends, your brain is still hardwired to cater for a large number of influences on your life. Therefore, when it comes to making decisions, chances are high that you will be making them based on other people's opinions, or on what you perceive others will think. This represents a double-edged sword; even though it can be good to get others' opinions when making a decision, it's these outside influences that can dramatically affect our ability to lead ourselves in making the right choices in life. If you can expose your child to situations where they can lead themselves in making decisions in the presence of others, better known as *social decisions*, your child will be in a much stronger position to be resilient to negative influences such as peer group pressure.

Troy and Shane were friends who had been in the same classes all through primary school and were now at high school together. Both boys were at a similar level academically, though Shane's grades had started slipping. Shane had fallen in with a bad crowd of students and was experimenting with drugs, while Troy had remained focused on his studies and avoided the bad influences. People often commented that Troy was more of a leader and Shane more of a follower, evident now in their response to their peer groups and attitudes to drugs. Troy refused drugs, even when it meant being ridiculed by others at school. But Shane liked being part of the gang, where he could blend in and not have to make decisions that could risk him being singled out.

Troy and Shane's story is a common one, and there are many possible factors at play as to why Troy was able to lead himself in making social decisions but Shane preferred to be led. However, when Troy was quizzed as to why there was a difference between them in making social decisions, he gave an interesting answer. He said that, unlike Shane, he'd always been encouraged to make his own decisions, even when it meant others might not approve. His parents always encouraged him to make decisions on behalf of the family, from where to set up the rug for a family picnic in the park to planning a family day trip. Troy described the worry of possibly getting his social decisions wrong and upsetting the family. But the more he was encouraged to make social decisions, the more he trusted his own judgement and the smaller the worry became. When things didn't go as well as Troy had hoped, he and everyone else in the family were able to manage the disappointment much better than he'd thought. In short, Troy knew to trust his ability to make effective social decisions, especially when he knew his decision to turn down drugs wouldn't be popular.

Problems that arise when children aren't allowed to lead

Arming your child with the ability to make effective social decisions so they can better manage the influence of peer pressure is a powerful gift. Unfortunately, children who don't have this ability to lead themselves, but are instead led by others, are more at risk of peer pressure. Common situations that peer pressure can lead young people into include:

* shoplifting
* using drugs and/or alcohol
* poor school performance
* vandalism or social deviancy.

Peer pressure is a real concern for any parent. How then can you help your child make good social decisions so they can better lead themselves when around others? Let your child take turns at leading the family. Here are some simple ways you can do this:

* Go exploring in the car and let your child determine which turns you should take (*Note:* make sure they know to give the driver plenty of notice for any directions).

* Go on a bushwalk or a walk around the street and let your child lead the way.

* Let your child choose which restaurant to get takeaway from (it may be worth giving them a small list of pre-determined options).

* When shopping, let your child choose a grocery item for the whole family, such as which box of tissues to buy (again, you might like to give your child two or three options to choose from).

After your child has made their social decision, praise them for it regardless of the outcome. Remember, there are no right or wrong answers with this exercise. Your aim is to help your child overcome the fear of making a wrong decision in the presence of others. If you can teach your child to lead themselves, they are more likely to make sound social decisions and better manage peer pressure. Remember, a good leader first leads themselves before leading others.

Summing up

Being allowed to lead the family can be very empowering for a child because you are teaching them that you trust their judgement. If you can empower your child to lead themselves in making social decisions, you are also teaching them to trust their own judgement, making them more resilient to peer group pressure. Starting today, how can you let your child lead?

14

CAN YOU HANDLE THE TRUTH?

'Exaggeration follows desperation.'

CHRIS BOWYER

In the film *A Few Good Men*, in response to Tom Cruise's statement, 'I want the truth', Jack Nicholson yells the famous quote, 'You can't handle the truth.' Unfortunately, many parents can't handle the truth either, especially when it comes from their own child.

Michael and his mother came into the counselling room for the first time and Michael's mum was extremely angry. The tension was incredible. She wanted Michael to admit to shoplifting a toy, even though he said his friend gave it to him. She said that Michael always lied to her. As we talked and emotions calmed, Michael's mother acknowledged that she was scared of being seen as a bad parent because of his behaviour. Michael in turn disclosed, to his mother's dismay, that he avoided telling her anything personal, including the truth, because he was scared of her reaction.

Parents want their children to tell them the truth. Yet, if the truth is something that upsets the parent dramatically, such as accidentally breaking a precious vase or scratching the family car, the child quickly learns that honesty isn't the best policy. A parent's inability to handle the truth unwittingly encourages the child to lie.

People often believe that lying starts in adolescence because young children are too innocent to carry out deceitful acts. Psychological studies aimed at detecting lying in children tell a different story. Children's lie-telling abilities emerge as early as three years of age and develop rapidly thereafter. From about the age of six a child is able to monitor what they say so that they don't leak the truth. One experiment involved asking three- to five-year-olds to guess what was under a cloth in front of them. Just before the investigator asked them for the answer, he got up and said that he just had to duck outside, but not to look under the cloth while he was gone. The child was being videotaped the whole time. When the interviewer came back, he asked the child if they had looked under the cloth. The younger children, unable to keep the lie going, quickly blurted out that they had looked. However, the older the child, the better their ability to conceal the truth and maintain a lie by saying they hadn't looked when they actually had.

Lying comes naturally to humans, and it starts being perfected in childhood. This doesn't mean that you should feel paranoid about how honest your child is. The reason for raising the issue is to highlight how important your response is when your child is honest with you, no matter how much you may dislike what they have to say. If your response to your child's honesty is negative, you are teaching your child to associate honesty with pain. Think about it, very few adults would be honest if it meant pain as a result.

Problems with your child lying to you

The main problem with a child who feels that they cannot be honest with their parent is that they are prevented from feeling that they can go to their parent for help when they are in a difficult situation, especially in adolescence. This could include having a fallout with a friend, damaging someone else's property, being in trouble with the law, owing someone money, teen pregnancy, contracting a sexually transmitted infection, or issues around drugs or alcohol. Many adults I see for counselling have major mental health issues because they have tried bottling up their emotions and keeping them hidden. Why? Because they have developed the belief, often in childhood, that others will think less of them if they reveal their emotions. Ironically, because these adults fear the consequences of being honest about their emotions, the avoidance keeps the anxiety or depression alive, preventing help being sought. The child who believes they can't be honest about their feelings is potentially being set up to follow a similar path as they move into adulthood.

How often have you heard of an adult whose life-threatening illness could have been treated if they'd sought help earlier? Or the person who loses everything because their pride wouldn't let them tell the bank of their financial situation? Or the one who injures themselves moving heavy objects because asking for help was not in their character? If you can allow your child to feel that they can ask for help when in trouble, you are giving them a vital safety skill that they'll take into adulthood. How can you create such an environment?

Creating an environment that supports honesty

I'm not advocating that you avoid punishing your child if they have done the wrong thing. It's important for a child to understand that there are consequences for their actions. What I *am* saying is that if your child does do the wrong thing and they tell you, then acknowledge how proud you are of them for being honest. From here, let them know that they'll still be punished, but that the punishment will be less than if you'd found out for yourself. However, *pause*

15

PUT IT OFF FOR LATER

'The ability to discipline yourself to delay gratification in the short term in order to enjoy greater rewards in the long term is the indispensable pre-requisite for success.'

BRIAN TRACY

If you give a child a lolly and they hold on to it without eating it straight away, they are more likely to develop into cognitively and socially competent adolescents, perform better at school, cope with frustration and stress, effectively pursue goals and resist temptation. This was the finding of a classic study by psychologists at Stanford University back in the 1960s, involving four-year-old preschool children. Each child was given a lolly, which they could eat if they wished. Here was the catch: the child was also told that if they didn't eat the lolly until the experimenter came back, they would be given extra lollies. The experimenter left the room and didn't return for some time. Some children couldn't hold on and ate the lolly, whereas those who could received extra lollies upon the experimenter's return. Some years later, the researchers followed up on the children and found that those who couldn't wait were more likely to have performed poorly at school, have lower paid jobs or be unemployed, and be less satisfied with the direction their life had taken. Conversely, those children who resisted the urge to eat the lolly until the researcher came back were more likely to have a higher level of education and better careers and be happier within themselves.

This study has since been supported by numerous follow-up studies and highlights how a child's level of self-control can help predict how successful and happy they'll be in later life. The take-home message is that if you can teach your child to wait for a reward, instead of needing it straight away, they are more likely to grow into successful, socially competent adults who are better able to cope with stress. Why then do parents often, generally unknowingly, teach their child instant gratification? The problem has a lot to do with modern times.

We live in a richer society than our parents did

Today's society generally has greater wealth than in previous generations, which doesn't provide a ready-made foundation for delayed gratification. This is because we are now in a better position to give our children what they demand. In years past, parents were unable to give children what they wanted because they simply couldn't afford it. So children were forced to wait for their birthdays or Christmas to receive that special toy, musical instrument or game they wanted. By having to wait, the child was inadvertently learning self-control through delayed gratification.

Now, not only do children have access to more materialistic possessions than any generation before them, but they also have access to a greater variety of things and at faster speeds. It takes less time to receive an email than a written letter; music can be bought online and downloaded immediately instead of having to physically visit a shop; and, thanks to mobile phones, friends can speak to each other virtually anywhere and anytime. How then can you teach your child self-control through delayed gratification in a society that promotes the complete opposite?

Teaching delayed gratification

You can teach your child delayed gratification in many different areas of their lives. Some of the ways you can show the power of waiting are:

* Have your child mark on a calendar the days until an exciting event, such as going on holidays.

* Have a set time that the TV is turned on and turned off, and stick to it.

* Allow your child to earn something they want instead of just buying it for them.

* When buying your child a treat, make a deal that they aren't allowed to eat it until you get to a pre-determined location, e.g. the park across the road from the shop.

* If you eat dinner at the table, ensure your child doesn't start eating until everyone is seated and the adults start first.

* Buy your child an ice-cream, but agree not to lick it until it has been paid for.

By delaying gratification in a controlled and psychologically safe way, you are teaching your child the valuable life skill of self-control. Be prepared, though: when teaching your child delayed gratification, they may initially protest. The trick here is to remember that this discomfort is normal and will soon pass. Another trick is to give your child options by letting them choose the outcome of a situation. For example, if you're shopping, give your child the choice of a smaller treat now or a much better one if they wait until you've finished shopping. If they choose the instant gratification and eat the treat now, but then later want the better treat as well, say no and stand firm. Remind your child that they had a choice and they chose the immediate treat. It may take a few tries, but your child will quickly learn not only that your word means something, but also that if they delay gratification, the reward will be bigger.

When I was a boy I desperately wanted a motorbike. My older brother had saved up and bought his own second-hand motorbike. Keen to have someone to ride with, he discovered that a neighbour was selling his mini-bike, which would have been perfect for me. After we begged my father, he agreed to buy me the bike on two conditions: firstly, I had to buy it myself, like my brother had, by earning money doing jobs around the house. My father would use the same approach as he had with my brother, matching me dollar for dollar, cent for cent for whatever money I earned. Knowing that $100 equated to $200 after my father matched me made saving for the motorbike excitingly achievable for my young mind. The second condition was that I wasn't allowed to ride the motorbike until it was fully paid for. The bike sat in the shed for months while I frantically earned money doing any jobs I could. At the time I quietly thought to myself that my parents would eventually give in and just give the bike to me. They didn't and, upon reflection, I'm glad as it was probably one of the greatest lessons they could have taught me.

Summing up

Teaching your child to wait before getting something they want is the key to success. Delay gratification wherever possible. Instead of letting your child eat their ice-cream straight after buying it, let the ice-cream melt just a little. By making your child wait just that little bit before getting what they want, you are cleverly teaching them to cope better with frustration and stress and to pursue their goals in effective ways. How can you teach your child about delayed gratification, starting today?

16

ENCOURAGE YOUR CHILD TO BE A PEOPLE-WATCHER

You can see a lot by observing.

YOGI BERRA

It's estimated that as much as 80 per cent of what a person communicates is through their body language. Being able to read another person's body language is a great skill to have and one that you can pass on to your child. A young person who isn't in tune with their own and other people's body language can risk getting people offside, as was the case with Harry.

Harry was a child who everyone wanted to avoid. Not because he was naughty or smelled bad, but because he talked too much. Once Harry engaged you in conversation, you couldn't escape. He was a normal, intelligent boy, but his parents were concerned about his lack of friends and brought him in to see me. What was interesting was that Harry himself knew that he talked too much, but said he couldn't tell when people had heard enough. It seemed that Harry wasn't picking up on other people's body language.

We organised for him to be filmed having conversations with other people, and then I taught Harry about body language. Once he had a basic understanding we then went back and watched the filmed conversations. Harry was initially excited that he could read the other people's body language, but was then horrified by what it was saying. By introducing Harry to body language, we provided a good inroad into working on other issues, such as his beliefs about himself and what others thought of him, as well as his communication skills.

Introducing young people to body language is a great way to develop their social skills. This is because it creates an awareness of other people's needs and wants. Also, by teaching your child about body language you will become more aware of your own. This is vital because, as a parent, you are always communicating with your child through your body language. Often it's when we are at our most stressed and have lost awareness of our own body language that we are communicating the most to our children.

Fortunately, reading body language is a skill that comes naturally to people. You can teach your child to develop their innate skill of reading others' body language by using the three activities below. I also recommend reading a book on body language with your child. Most libraries or bookshops will be able to recommend suitable titles. Generally these types of books are short reads packed with illustrations, as reading body language is visual.

Activity 1: Watch silent television

Young people can often be distracted by someone's words when learning to read their body language. The easiest way to get around this is to sit down with your child and watch television together. The only catch is that the television's sound must be turned off. This way both you and your child can try to work out what is happening with the characters on television without hearing them talk. Learning to read others' body language by watching silent television avoids everyday distractions so your child can focus on the task at hand. This activity is a great game, and children learn best when they're having fun.

Activity 2: Role-play emotions

The following activity may be a little more challenging for your child, though they should be a lot more comfortable with the idea of reading body language after doing the silent television activity above. Start by acting out different emotions to your child through your body language for them to guess how you are feeling. The rule is that the person acting out the emotions is not allowed to speak. Express different facial and body stances such as stress, surprise, shyness, happiness, sadness, confidence, anger and so on. Once you feel your child has mastered reading your body language, swap roles so they act out different emotions for you to guess. Not only is it good for your child to be able to read others' body language, but it's also vital for them to have an understanding of how they themselves are communicating to others. Again, make it fun – it can be a game of charades, which all kids love!

Activity 3: People-watch in real life

Once the two previous activities have been played and you feel your child has a good understanding of body language, you can take them out into the real world to practise their people-watching skills. Go to a public place such as a large shopping mall and, as inconspicuously as possible, watch other people interact. Please note, it's advisable to encourage your child to be as subtle as possible and to make sure you choose to look at people who appear non-threatening. Generally, people don't mind a child staring but may get the wrong idea if another adult does. Therefore, keep your own glances short.

As you're doing these three activities, you want to be getting your child's feedback about what they are seeing.

That way you can praise or offer feedback on any of their observations. This will help finetune their people-watching skills.

Summing up

Body language is a great skill for both you and your child to have. It will help you become aware of what you are communicating to your child, and will also provide a great inroad for your child to develop their social skills. When helping your child develop their body-language reading skills, patiently ask what they are observing so you can praise or correct any beliefs they have. Above all else, reading body language should be fun, so make a game out of it with your child.

17

BE A PIONEER PARENT

'Be the kind of person you always wanted your parents to be.'

CAR BUMPER STICKER

We like to think that we are free thinkers. However, many of us rarely question our own beliefs or where they have come from. This is especially true in the case of parenting.

Clare was in the kitchen helping her mum prepare Christmas lunch for all the family who had come over to visit. As Clare's mum went to put the turkey in the oven, Clare asked why it had been cut in half. Baffled, Clare's mum couldn't answer and said it had been something that her mother had always done. Clare's grandma was laying the table in the next room so both Clare and her mum asked her why she used to cut the turkey in half. She gave a similar baffled response as Clare's mum, couldn't explain why, and said it was something that her mother had always done. Clare's great-grandma was sitting in the lounge room, so Clare, her mother and grandma all went and asked why she used to cut the turkey in half. Upon hearing the question, Clare's great-grandmother smiled and said that the oven she had at the time was too small to house a full turkey and cutting it in half was the only way it would fit.

If Clare had not questioned why the turkey had been cut in half, this unspoken tradition would have most likely been carried on for a fourth consecutive generation. In the past, people rarely questioned their parents' beliefs towards raising children. As there was little information about positive ways of parenting, new parents had to rely largely on using their parents as role models, which often involved unconsciously copying their beliefs.

Below are some unquestioned truths around parenting. Have you heard or experienced any of them?

* 'I was belted as a child and it hasn't done *me* any harm.'

* 'It's the mother's job, not the father's, to take care of a child's emotional needs.'

* 'Children get over things more easily than adults.'

* 'Children are too young to understand adult worries, so they're not affected by them.'

Before you panic about the possibility of copying the negative aspects of your own parents' parenting style (something you swore you'd never do), know that a child copying their parents' actions and beliefs is a normal human survival skill. However, what you need to do now is determine if the parenting style that was modelled to you is going to be the most helpful for your child. This will require following three simple steps.

Step 1: Have the courage to feel guilt about questioning your parents

The first step in breaking unhelpful family beliefs around parenting is to question the parenting style or beliefs that were passed down to you. Rest assured, you can do this without having to confront your parents. Even so, it can still trigger feelings of guilt and betrayal. In the past, children were taught never to question their parents, and if they did they were considered rude, disobedient and disloyal. So when you question your parents' beliefs, it's perfectly normal to feel guilty. Just acknowledge the guilty feelings to yourself. This guilt shows you are stepping out of a comfort zone and improving your own parenting. Added to this, by admitting to yourself that you feel guilt, these feelings will quickly dissipate. Often it is trying to avoid or ignore the feeling that keeps the guilt going strong.

This exercise is not designed to be an attack against your parents. Neither your parents, nor any generation before them, had access to the quality of parenting research and information that you have access to today. You are questioning the parenting techniques used on you *not* as a form of disloyalty to your parents, but as a way of best helping your child.

What if there is pain in reflecting?

Many parents have had traumatic childhoods, and this often acts as a motivator to ensure their own children never go through what they did. If you find the pain too great trying to reflect on your own childhood then I strongly encourage you to seek professional help so they can help you work through it. The reason for dealing with a painful past, instead of trying to bury or ignore it, is that generally the more a person tries to ignore or avoid a certain discomfort, the more they will be attracted to it. Psychologists have found that trying to block something from the mind not only takes a lot of energy, but it also inadvertently makes that issue the focus of your attention. This is because the painful thought, memory or belief has to be at the front of one's mind so it can be guarded against the moment it is thought about. It's a bit like being told not to think of a pink elephant. To understand the command, you first have to think of a pink elephant. In short, trying to ignore something usually makes it worse.

Step 2: Knowing what to keep and what to reject

To be a pioneer parent you have to adopt the helpful beliefs your parents held about parenting and reject those that aren't helpful. In order to do this, you need to create an awareness of how you were parented. As the saying goes, 'Those that don't understand history are condemned to repeat it.' To help create this awareness, try answering the following list of questions and think about whether the techniques your parents used were positive or negative.

* Did your parents openly encourage you to express your emotions or to keep them bottled up?

* Were you praised for trying or only when you achieved?

* Did you feel your parents' love and support were unconditional or dependent on certain things?

* What do you do or say that your parents did that you swore you would never do as a parent yourself?

* How did your parents show they loved you? (Hugs and kisses versus buying material objects such as toys.)

* Were your parents' discipline measures appropriate? And was it your behaviour that was punished or your self-worth – 'Because you didn't listen, you're not getting dessert tonight' versus 'You're a worthless kid who never listens'.

* Did you feel like you were listened to, in particular your concerns?

* Could you be honest with your parents or did you lie or keep things hidden for fear of their response?

* Were you treated as an equal in the family?

How did you go? Were you able to uncover ways your parents handled things that affected their parenting skills in either a positive or a negative way? If so, well done. If not then I encourage you to either try again later or discuss it with a trusted person. Remember, your aim is to implement the positive techniques your parents used and eliminate the negative ones.

Step 3: Be prepared for a backlash

As you develop new parenting techniques as a result of questioning the way you were parented, you might find that those close to you object to your new parenting style. Why? People naturally resist change because it can seem threatening, even if it's change for the better. Being a pioneer in any area is uncomfortable – you are creating your own new path and not following the crowd. Just keep your child's best interests in mind, knowing that others will soon become accustomed to your changes. It's like seeing a friend's new hairstyle for the first time – initially it may throw you, but it won't be long before you get used to it.

If you feel that your parents' approach to raising children wasn't helpful, but that you haven't adopted any of their ways, I encourage you to think again. Many parents I've seen for counselling who have had painful upbringings have told me through clenched teeth that they'll never be cranky and aggressive like their parents were to them. A mirror would show them otherwise: they have unknowingly adopted the anger that they were so adamant they had avoided. As sure as the sun rises and sets, we have all picked up traits from our parents that will influence our parenting. Some of these traits will be easy to identify, though many will hide under the surface. I urge you to take the time to uncover these traits by following the suggestions outlined in this chapter. Your child's happiness is counting on it.

Summing up

Humans are creatures of habit, and generally we parent the way we were parented. It takes courage to question the beliefs towards child raising your parents unknowingly passed on to you. Becoming aware of your own parenting style in relation to the way you were parented better enables you to adopt what was helpful and reject what wasn't. Let what's best for your child guide and motivate you to start breaking unhelpful generational parenting beliefs. Teach your child that they don't have to follow the crowd by showing them that you are a pioneer parent.

18

DARE TO LOOK IN THE MIRROR

'What if the question is not why
am I so infrequently the person
I really want to be, but why do I so
infrequently want to be the person
I really am?'

ORIAH MOUNTAIN DREAMER

As adults, we are often terrified of our own reflection. Seeing ourselves in photos or video footage can be very uncomfortable. However, this discomfort is compounded exponentially when it comes to looking at ourselves as a parent. I have counselled many parents who blame everyone and everything except themselves when trying to explain their child's bad behaviour.

Penny took her nine-year-old son, Kyle, to countless medical professionals to fix his bad behaviour. Whether it was medication prescribed from doctors or naturopaths, healing crystals, acupuncture, cleansing diets, new teachers, new schools, counselling, chiropractic spinal realignment or even hypnosis, Penny had taken Kyle to see everyone. Those who suggested that Penny's anxiety was at the centre of Kyle's naughtiness were promptly struck off the list and a new professional was sought. However, it was Kyle's new soccer coach who made an inroad. One day after a soccer match, he took Penny aside and disclosed that he used to suffer from anxiety until he got help. He then suggested that she herself see someone for counselling. Amazingly, Penny did and as a result learned that she suffered from anxiety. Once Penny started working on her own issues, Kyle's behaviour quickly started to improve.

It is stories like Penny's that strike fear in most parents' hearts. Why? Because often upon reading this story a parent instantly starts questioning if they are a bad parent too. I'm not here to push guilt trips about the quality of your parenting. There are no perfect parents out there, myself included. Yet not being willing to stand back and honestly look at the way we are parenting – not seeing what influence we are having on our child – is a recipe for disaster for our children's wellbeing.

Why do parents avoid the mirror?

Why do so many parents resist looking at themselves and instead lay blame on other people or things? In one word: pain. Fear of failure as a parent is a powerful motivator because it brings with it psychological pain. Many parents unknowingly deceive themselves into thinking that if they can avoid looking in the mirror, they won't be to blame and will avoid feeling psychological pain. This is what psychologists call self-deception.

What is self-deception?

It has been said that self-deception is a lie without a liar. It is our natural psychological safeguard that protects our self-esteem from the harsh truth of reality. Self-deception achieves this by tricking a person into not having accurate insights into their own limitations. Studies on self-deception show that as humans we naturally:

* take undue credit for lucky accomplishments

* overestimate the number of other people who share our beliefs

* fail to recognise our self-inflicted failures

* perceive illusory relationships between events that aren't related, such as believing it's only raining because you're on holidays

* falsely believe that the qualities that make us desirable are unique to ourselves.

Even though self-deception helps maintain a person's self-esteem, and we need a certain degree of self-deception to remain happy, it prevents a person from seeing their bad habits and correcting them. When it comes to parenting, bad habits are fuelled by self-deception. Don't be fooled; just because self-deception will make you feel temporarily better by justifying your parenting actions, and avoiding psychological pain, ultimately it is your child who will be the most negatively affected.

Below are some examples of parents' bad habits that are disguised by self-deception:

* 'Sure, I may shout a lot at my child, but I've never physically hurt them.'

* 'Children should know that parents can't keep all their promises.'

* 'Compared to other parents, I'm definitely better than most.'

* 'I push my child to be their best in everything they do so they'll have a secure future.'

* 'I work long hours so I can afford to give my child all the things I never had when I was young.'

Self-deception allows a person to maintain bad habits because it refutes any evidence that clashes with the person's beliefs about themselves and seeks out facts to confirm them. For example, a child's sporting coach warns the parent of pushing the child too hard. Yet the parent tells the coach that they know what's best for their child and they are only pushed because they can cope with it.

If a parent suspects that self-deception may be hindering their parenting, what can be done? The way to combat self-deception is to become aware of how you deal with information that conflicts with how you see yourself as a parent. You can improve your parenting by taking a page out of an elite performer's book. How is it that a gold medallist ice-skater falls more in practice than other skaters at lower ability levels? Surely the more accomplished the ice-skater, the less frequently they should be falling, right? Wrong! Research into elite athletes shows that they make far more mistakes practising than athletes not quite at their level of ability. Why? Elite athletes practise the parts they aren't confident about, whereas the average grade athlete will focus on practising the parts they know.

How can you apply this to improving your parenting skills? Once a person has attained a certain level of proficiency in their area of expertise, such as parenting, it's only through feedback about their weaker areas that they can improve. This means that even though compliments about your parenting are nice, they alone won't make you a better parent. What you need is to honestly look at your parenting to see if there is anywhere you can improve. This may not be as easy as it sounds because of that pesky psychological safeguard, self-deception.

For the rest of this chapter, as you read, ask yourself, 'What am I doing with the information that conflicts with the beliefs I hold about my parenting?'

Looking past self-deception

Building on the previous chapter, you need to honestly assess your own parenting and find areas that can be refined. If you're feeling uncomfortable just at the thought of this, then you're in the majority. I know I myself find this exercise initially difficult, though the benefit that comes from using it, and using it often, is amazing. Here is a list of questions that will help you get started in uncovering hidden bad habits so you can change them. They may prompt you to think of some others – remember no one's perfect so be kind to yourself as you read ahead:

* Are you able to accept responsibility for your child's bad behaviour, or do you always put the blame on them or others?

* Do you take too much responsibility for your child and stop them from having freedom that is appropriate for their age?

* Do you have a sore throat or headache at the end of the day from continually disciplining your child?

* Do you always tell your child you will play with them later, but never seem to get around to it?

How did you go? Were you able to uncover areas that need improvement? If you did, well done. If you didn't, I encourage you to try again at a later date. When a parent tells me that they are doing everything right, I panic. Once you have discovered an area of your parenting that is weak, you can start taking small steps towards refining it to the way you want it to be. This can take a little time so be patient. Generally, though, once a weaker area is brought to a person's attention and the self-deception is lifted, the problem fixes itself. A problem gains strength by being hidden.

Summing up

Teaching your child to be confident first comes through leading by example. Muster up the courage to look at yourself in the mirror to see what your parenting is like and where it can be improved. By lifting the guard of self-deception, we are better able to address the parts of our parenting style that need finetuning. This can be a terrifying thought, though nothing can be improved unless it is first identified. It takes courage to look honestly at our weaker points and be willing to improve them. This is why there are a lot of people who are average at chosen tasks, but very few who are exceptionally good. Become the best parent you can be by discovering and then working on your weaker points. Go on, dare to look in the mirror.

19

LET YOUR CHILD EAVESDROP

*'If you want your children to improve,
let them overhear the nice things you
say about them to others.'*

HAIM GINOTT

One of the best ways to give a person a compliment is to give one indirectly. Have you ever tried to give someone a compliment, only to find they dismiss it? Some people feel uncomfortable and try to dismiss it in an attempt to manage their social discomfort. Having your compliment rejected is like a slap in the face – by knocking back your compliment, the person is unknowingly saying that you are wrong. If someone gives you a compliment you should accept it graciously. That way you are returning the compliment.

Even though children readily lap up praise, at times they can question the authenticity of it. This doesn't mean that you should stop giving positive feedback to your child – children who aren't praised or positively encouraged generally have low self-esteem. But it can be a powerful boost to your child's courage levels if you occasionally vary the way you give them a compliment. How can you do this? Involve a third person when giving your child a compliment.

Research shows that if you pass on someone else's compliment, the person receiving the compliment is less likely to knock it back. Why? Because you didn't give the compliment, you were just the messenger. Passing on a compliment gets past a person's defence mechanisms, making them more likely to believe what you say and see you as a good person.

Another way to use this principle with your child is to let them overhear you tell someone else about something positive your child has done. By doing so you are making a public declaration to others that you believe in your child. This is a sure-fire way of giving their self-esteem an almighty boost. Some examples of positive statements are:

* 'I was so proud of the way my son, Gavin, handled his soccer team being runners-up in the grand final.'

* 'I saw Kimberly's painting and thought to myself, "At last we have an artist in the family."'

* 'You should have seen how well Emmy danced at her school concert recently. All the practice she put in really showed.'

* 'I was initially scared about David learning to ride a bike, but seeing how quickly he picked it up, I had nothing to worry about.'

The aim is to praise your child to another adult about something your child feels they have genuinely achieved. This way they will link their actions with success, thereby fostering self-confidence. This may sound boastful, but it's all about balance. It only takes your child overhearing one small compliment from you to have the desired effect.

Summing up

Keep praising your child, but occasionally vary the way you deliver a compliment. Do this by telling a third person about something great your child has done so that your child can overhear the conversation. This is a potent way of nurturing your child's self-confidence. What has your child done well lately that you can tell someone else about?

20

FIND THINGS TO TALK ABOUT

'The way you overcome shyness is to become so wrapped up in something that you forget to be afraid.'

LADY BIRD JOHNSON

Terry's parents came to me for counselling because they were extremely worried about their young son's apparent shyness around others. Terry would initially stand back when meeting new children instead of getting in and playing. Once he had been around these children for a little while, he would start interacting with them more. He also hated giving speeches in class and became tongue-tied when trying to talk to adults. Terry's parents kept telling him that there was nothing to be scared of, and his father's advice was always the same: 'People won't bite you.' They couldn't understand why their son was initially so hesitant to play with children he didn't know. However, the more we talked, the more it became apparent that there were two sets of rules, one for Terry's parents and another for Terry. Both parents agreed that they themselves wouldn't go to a social event with other adults and instantly be the life of the party. Terry's father also confessed that he hated picking Terry up from school because he'd have to interact with the other parents and he never knew what to say. Terry's parents highlight a common misconception held by adults – that children shouldn't be nervous in social situations, but it is different if adults are.

Public speaking isn't technically our number one fear, though it is a good representation of it. Our number one fear is rejection by others. Fear of rejection is even greater than the fear of dying. This is because our early ancestors lived in small clans or tribes, and to be rejected and kicked out of the clan would have meant certain death. Therefore it was in a person's best interests to keep the peace and not to upset those around them. Interestingly, even though we no longer live in clans or tribes, the fear of rejection is hardwired in our brains and affects everything we do, from the clothes we wear to the houses we live in, the friends we have, the cars we drive, the deodorant we wear and even to the best example of all, the clothes we iron, which is done purely for other people's opinion of us. We are unconsciously ruled by the fear of external criticism.

Our fear of rejection can cause us to be constantly on guard when around others, even in seemingly harmless social situations. But we all have to learn to manage this fear so that we can lead positive and fulfilling lives. We need to manage this fear in many situations, from job interviews to choosing a partner. If a person doesn't learn to manage this fear they set themselves up for a very anxious or lonely life. How can you help your child to better handle this innate fear of social interactions? You develop your child's conversation confidence and teach them to find interesting topics to talk about.

Having a conversation with someone you wouldn't normally talk to can be a scary prospect for any person, let alone a child. Fear of saying something stupid or not saying anything at all and embarrassing oneself is a very real concern for a lot of us. This is why so many people don't say anything in social situations unless the conversation is initiated by another. What makes a person a good conversationalist? Studies show that together with good listening skills, good conversationalists have developed a string of 'topics' to have flexibility in initiating different types of conversations to suit the situation. Help develop your child's conversation confidence by coming up with a short list of topics together to initiate conversations with other children. Common topics children love to talk about include:

* complaining about school (teachers/homework) or parents

* movies

* siblings

* music

* the internet.

To get ideas for other topics, encourage your child to do some research and listen in on other children talking to see what's popular. (*Note:* Warn your child about subtlety here – you don't want them to seem smothering.) It's not until we are made aware of something new that we start noticing it – when you buy a car you notice all the same models as yours on the road. By teaching your child to look out for things to talk about, you will help broaden their awareness about other people's wants. This is the key attribute of good conversationalists: they are interested in other people and want to know all about them. Their focus is on the person they are talking to instead of just on themselves. Shy or introverted people tend to focus more on themselves and the way they think they are coming across to others. These types of people often try to cut themselves off from the external world because they don't know how to interact with it. Encouraging your child to develop their awareness in finding conversation topics will help put their focus more on things external to them and less on themselves.

Once you have your conversation topics, we will look at applying them in the following chapter.

Summing up

Our number one fear is rejection by others; our brains are hardwired for it. This is why it's normal for your child to feel a bit nervous about interacting with other people they wouldn't normally speak to. A key to managing this anxiety and developing conversation confidence is having things to talk about. By exposing your child to different conversation topics, you're developing their ability to adapt to different personalities when having a conversation. Being able to tailor the conversation topic to the individual person they are speaking to at the time is a key ingredient of a good conversationalist.

21

HELP DEVELOP 'CONVERSATION CONFIDENCE'

'Confidence contributes more to conversation than wit.'

FRANÇOIS DE LA ROCHEFOUCAULD (1613–1680)

We all respond automatically to the fear of rejection, with clear signs of it developing in children as young as two years of age. One possible response to the threat of rejection is blushing, as it only occurs in response to social attention. Interestingly, even though humans are the only animal that blush, psychologists don't really know why, but suspect blushing may act as a public signal to others of our distress and non-threatening intentions.

Matilda, a six-year-old, came to me because she was very shy. Whenever I asked her a question, she would look blank and then turn to her mum. Her mother would then respond by speaking for Matilda as she knew her daughter would not talk and would probably blush. I later explained that as long as she was Matilda's interpreter, there was no reason for her to speak to adults. Matilda's mum changed this, and it wasn't long before Matilda was explaining to me why she had to cut her Barbie doll's hair off. Once she was given the opportunity to speak in a safe environment, she came out of her shell.

After developing the conversation topics from the previous chapter, it's now time to test them by helping your child have a conversation in a safe environment. Naturally, this will have to be with someone other than you. A simple way of creating a safe environment for your child to speak is to start up a conversation together with a trusted person such as an extended family member, friend or neighbour. The trick is for you to initiate the conversation by talking about something great your child has done, for instance, 'We are very proud of [your child's name] because he/she did [something good]. Why don't you tell them about it, [your child's name]?'

Once you have started the conversation for your child, step back and let them take over. This way, your child can then make a safe entry into the conversation. It's here that it's vital to support your child instead of rescuing them. Many parents feel the need to jump in and talk for their child, especially if they are struggling for a word or taking too long to tell the story. All this is doing is reaffirming that they are inept in social interactions. If the urge to jump in and speak for your child strikes you, first count to ten before talking. The more practice your child has, the better they will become at interacting with others and the less you will feel the need to jump in and rescue them.

After the conversation, praise your child for their courage in speaking to an adult. Remember, start with both a topic and a person your child feels comfortable with. Otherwise, you risk throwing them in the deep end of the pool and shattering their confidence.

Once you and your child have practised having conversations with trusted people and they appear comfortable, it's time to have them initiate a conversation with a stranger. Now, if you're like most parents, your 'stranger danger' alarm will probably be activated just by the thought of your child talking to a stranger. You can help them by choosing a safe stranger in a safe and comfortable setting. A good way to help your child develop their conversation confidence is to use the phone. Practise with your child what they will say and then, once comfortable, have them phone up a child-friendly business to:

* find out what their opening hours are
* see if they have a certain product in stock,
  e.g. a movie at the video store
* order takeaway food.

When initiating conversations, encourage your child to rate their discomfort, both before and after making the call, and write it down in a notebook. This way your child will be able to see their progress. Seeing progress is a powerful motivator for anyone, especially children. Remember, praise your child after each call, no matter how small the step. If your child picks up the phone and speaks, that's progress. You may even establish with your child a reward they can have if they make a certain number of phone calls. If your child is very anxious, reward them after the first phone call.

If your child refuses to make the call, ask them for help in finding the phone numbers for the places you are going to call. Involving them in the process will help them take ownership of the challenge. Then phone one of the businesses on your list while your child is next to you. This way you will be modelling to them what to ask on the phone. Also, make sure the phone numbers are for places that would interest your child. Generally, finding out the opening hours of a toyshop will be far more appealing than finding out the opening hours for the dentist.

Talk to an adult face to face

Your final task is for your child to initiate a conversation with an adult face to face. This can be done by having your child invite a school friend over to play. Organise it first with the parent of your child's friend. Explain to the parent that you're working on developing your child's confidence with conversations and check that it's okay if your child does the asking in regards to the play date. Once this has been arranged, explain to your child that they need to ask their friend's parent about the play date. Reassure them that you'll be there when they ask. Use exactly the same principles as you have done with the exercises above. Remember, go at your child's pace and praise any step they make, no matter how small.

Initiate a conversation topic

Assuming your child has tried the above exercises and been able to manage their anxiety, they are now ready to put their conversation topics to the test. This can be approached in a few ways. Your child can either choose someone their own age, like a student at school, or a safe adult who is easy to approach, such as a neighbour or extended family member. Plan with your child who they will start up a conversation with. Once they have agreed on a person, practise with them the topics that they are going to initiate. Make sure this preparation is light and fun; if you create a serious atmosphere where it feels like they are going into battle, it's unlikely they'll follow through and do it. Their goal in initiating a conversation is to simply ask the person a question. They may ask a student at school what they think of all the homework they get or they may ask a neighbour how their pet is going. If more conversation develops from this, that's great. However, their main goal is to just ask one simple question.

Summing up

Our brains are wired to respond to the fear of rejection. Therefore it's natural if your child feels apprehensive about initiating conversations. Support them through this by choosing social challenges you feel your child can handle. As you start small and build the difficulty level over time, be mindful of resisting the temptation to jump in and rescue your child by talking for them. Give your child room to find and develop their own conversation confidence. Starting today, who could you use to help develop your child's conversation confidence?

22

QUESTION TV IN FRONT OF YOUR CHILD

'Don't you wish there were a knob on the TV to turn up the intelligence. There's one marked "Brightness" but it doesn't work.'

(LEO ANTHONY) GALLAGHER

Due to a child's developing brain, they often think that what's on TV is a true representation of reality. This can be of concern when research suggests that the average child will have watched:

* at least 13,000 hours of TV, or a full 1½ years, twenty-four hours a day, by the time they have graduated from high school

* several thousand murders on TV before reaching adolescence
* one violent act against another person approximately every three minutes while watching an average children's cartoon.

Added to this, studies show that:

* boys watch more TV than girls
* children with lower IQs watch more TV than those with higher IQs
* children from lower income families watch more TV than children from higher income families.

The reason for highlighting these issues is not for you to feel you have to ban your child from watching TV. That's not my intention at all. Instead I'd like you to see TV as a learning device. And like many electronic learning tools, TV can be both potentially beneficial for academic and social learning and destructive in promoting unhealthy and terrifying beliefs about the world. Children are brilliant observers but can be poor interpreters of events that are beyond their level of understanding. This is because of their developing brains. Therefore, as a parent, it's important to help your child process what they see and hear on television. Otherwise, your child might develop a seriously distorted view of reality, setting them up for mental health issues such as anxiety disorders.

Talisha was a young child who suddenly refused to go out in the backyard. She had always loved playing on the trampoline and in the sandpit but now she would burst into tears if her mum tried to make her go out there. Feeling both puzzled and distressed, Talisha's mum sat down with her and quietly asked what was wrong with the backyard. Talisha finally confided that she was scared of the rocks. Talisha's mum resisted the urge to dismiss her fear and instead asked more questions. It turned out that Talisha had watched a supposedly innocent cartoon where the main characters were suddenly attacked by giant rocks with large teeth and beady eyes. Talisha was now scared that those same rocks would be in her backyard. Talisha's mum went to work correcting her daughter's belief by looking closely at many of the rocks in the backyard with her and patiently noting that they didn't have any teeth or eyes, that they were not living and that many of the things on TV are not real. Eventually Talisha went outside, holding her mother's hand, and inspected the backyard. It wasn't long before she realised that it was safe again, quickly forgot about the rock monsters and got back to playing.

A classic cause of anxiety issues such as phobias is watching scary TV shows, especially at a young age. Some parents believe it's okay to let their child watch terrifying horror movies, because the parent knows the movies are not real. Films that are notoriously responsible for developing phobias in people include *The Birds*, *Jaws*, *Arachnophobia*, *IT* (horror movie involving a murdering clown) and *Indiana Jones* (both the snake and spider scenes). In Talisha's case, if her belief about rock monsters, picked up from watching a cartoon, had not been challenged and handled so respectfully by her mother, Talisha could have been on the path to developing an anxiety disorder. It can be that easy.

So choose what TV shows you expose your child's mind to with care. Here are some suggested guidelines you might consider applying to your child's TV watching:

* Have absolute rules both about the amount of TV viewing time a day and the programs watched.

* Encourage your child to know what they want to watch before turning on the TV, thereby avoiding the trap of just watching whatever's on at the time.

* Where possible, watch TV with your child and discuss the programs (even watching a minute or two of each program will give you a feel for what's happening).

* Throw away the remote to avoid flipping through channels mindlessly and instead encourage your child to watch the TV deliberately and selectively.

* Lead by example and display good TV habits
  yourself.

What if your child is watching TV and you notice that the program is displaying inappropriate behaviour, clothing or language? If you don't feel it's bad enough to turn the channel, it's important that you express your disapproval and explain to your child why. For example, if a cartoon character gets shot, falls off a cliff or has something large dropped on them and then recovers by merely shaking themselves (typical scenes in many Bugs Bunny and Road Runner cartoons), point out to your child that this wouldn't happen in real life and explain why. If possible, suggest a better way of dealing with the situation. Where language or attitude is degrading or bratty, label this and ask your child what would happen if they themselves spoke to an adult like that. It's important that your child knows there is more than one way to deal with a situation, especially if it's resolving conflict.

You will be walking a fine line here – you don't want to come across as a nagger or a party pooper by insulting your child's TV show characters, as you'll likely be asked to leave the room. So be subtle. Remember, if a show is not suitable, don't let your child watch it. However, if the show *is* suitable but sometimes the characters say or do slightly questionable things, just discrediting the authenticity of a

TV scene with a few words can be enough to plant a seed in your child's mind against forming unrealistic beliefs about the world.

Summing up

Television can be a great learning tool and can give parents a well-needed break. It also has the danger of shaping unrealistic beliefs in your child's developing mind. Therefore, police your child's TV watching. If possible, tape appropriate TV shows so they can be watched when nothing suitable is on. Also, try to watch TV programs with your child and correct any untruths you see, explaining why these events wouldn't actually occur in real life.

23

AVOID THE IQ TRAP

'It's not how smart you are, it's how you are smart!'

HOWARD GARDNER (PSYCHOLOGIST)

A child who completes an intelligence (IQ) test generally has to wait at least nine months before they can be retested. Why? Psychologists call it 'practice effect'. Whatever task the human brain does, it naturally looks for and remembers patterns in an effort to make the next attempt easier. Once a person knows the underlying structure of a psychological test, the test loses its effectiveness. Psychological tests definitely have their place, but resting a child's future on it can be a grave mistake, as I learned from experience.

Halfway through high school, I had no idea what I wanted to do for a career. This worried my parents; they thought that if I had a career to aim for, I'd apply myself more at school. So my mother had me professionally assessed to determine what careers would best suit my personality. I was given an IQ test along with a string of other psychological tests one after another over several hours, without a break. After paying a large sum of money that my parents couldn't really afford, we were given the results with a list of recommended careers for me. I was gently advised to avoid university or anything academic, and to stick to careers that better suited my strengths, such as manual work. I have nothing against manual work, but what scares me is that for years it was all I focused on because I thought it was all I could do. It wasn't until years later that I considered going against the 'manual labour' label I'd been given and enrolled in university to become a psychologist. The only reason I wanted to be a psychologist was a selfish one: I wanted to fix the phobia of medical procedures I had developed after undergoing a traumatic operation without anaesthetic in a third-world hospital.

If I had been led by my IQ scores as a young adult, I would never have become a psychologist, nor would I have written books, both of which give me a deep sense of personal satisfaction. The reason IQ tests can be so potentially damaging is that psychologists are discovering that they don't represent a person's full intelligence. Some psychologists say that IQ tests are designed to weed out the creative people. This is because IQ tests can't measure originality, creativity, artistic and musical talent, leadership qualities, people skills or the ability to control one's own emotions. These variables are now being classed as emotional intelligence. Yet in our society, especially in the education system, IQ scores still set the benchmark as to how smart someone is. We think that unless our child is in the top class at school for maths, English or science, it spells disaster for their future. But there are many roads to success. Here is a list of some famous people who either dropped out of their educational studies or failed:

* Boris Becker (three-time Wimbledon champion)

* Sean Connery (Oscar-winning actor)

* Michael Dell (founder of Dell Computers)

* Jane Austen (novelist)

* Sir Elton John (musician)

* Bill Gates (richest man in the world and founder of Microsoft)

* Whoopi Goldberg (actress)

* Peter Jackson (Oscar-winning film director–writer–producer of *The Lord of the Rings* trilogy)

* Billy Joel (musician)

* Calvin Klein (fashion designer).

The area in which these people excelled was emotional intelligence. But emotions tend to be seen as a sign of weakness and we are encouraged to try to ignore them. Encouraging your child to ignore their emotions won't make the feelings go away. Instead the emotions get bottled up. Because children don't have the brain development to instantly identify and make sense of their emotions, especially the painful ones, these unnamed feelings can be terrifying and can ultimately lower self-confidence. Not identifying their emotions can lead to children avoiding certain situations, people or things. However, when a child is assisted by an adult to put a name to their emotions, especially the painful ones, it allows them to make sense of their world and regain a sense of control. In short, they are being encouraged to develop their emotional intelligence.

How can you help develop your child's emotional intelligence? The best way is to become an 'emotion coach' by first getting to know your own emotions.

Be an 'emotion coach'

Many adults are terrified of their emotions and try to avoid them by doing such things as drinking alcohol, burying themselves in work, smoking, impulse shopping, watching too much TV or eating to excess. So if you're now having reservations about your suitability as a role model for your child, don't worry. By simply getting to know your own emotions, you will in turn help your child get to know theirs. Believe it or not, it actually takes more effort to try to ignore and bottle up one's emotions than to get to know them. Research shows that the five ways you can be a good emotion role model are to:

1. **BE AWARE OF EVEN LOW-INTENSITY EMOTIONS IN YOURSELF** Model labelling your emotions to specific situations in front of your child. For example: I'm feeling happy because I finished the crossword; I'm feeling sad that the pet goldfish died; I'm feeling upset that you didn't take your muddy shoes off outside the house. Identifying and labelling your emotions in front of your child will teach them how to label theirs. *Note:* If a parent only labels their emotions of anger because of something the child has done, there's a good chance that there are bigger issues at work than just the child's behaviour. It may be worth chatting to a close friend or seeking professional help.

2. **SEE YOUR CHILD'S NEGATIVE EMOTIONS AS AN OPPORTUNITY** Many adults see a child's negative emotions – anger, fear, guilt, embarrassment and sadness – as problems to eliminate, rather than an opportunity. Even though this is true in part, these negative emotions also provide the greatest inroad

to developing your child's emotional intelligence. If these emotions are misunderstood, they will cause a child great distress. If your child can understand and manage their negative emotions, emotions we all have, they will be able to understand themselves better and manage their own actions. So, for instance, if your child is being silently cranky, coach them through how to handle themselves by first seeing the negative emotion as a platform for helping your child develop. This will take courage on your part not to react instantly. Instead breathe, and pause before punishing. This will place you in a better position to move to the next step.

3. **ASSIST YOUR CHILD IN VERBALLY LABELLING THEIR EMOTIONS** Remember your child will find it initially difficult to label their emotions. Assist them by suggesting the emotion they may be feeling and enquiring about its possible cause. For example: 'You sound angry. Is it because you can't get your toy to work?' Putting a name to the emotion as well as a possible cause removes the guesswork for your child about their emotional status, which in turn helps empower them. Even if your child doesn't understand at first, that's fine. The more often you label their emotions, the more they will see the connection between their emotions and their behaviour.

4. **LISTEN TO YOUR CHILD'S CONCERNS** Ask your child what is bothering them and then *listen* with genuine concern. Resist rushing to extract information from them, and instead go at their pace. Showing empathy and validating the emotions your child is experiencing can be extremely comforting as it helps them feel normal. For example: 'I can see why you're upset that you weren't able to ride your scooter to the shops by yourself. I remember my parents doing similar things for my own safety when I was young, and I hated it.' The rule here is to make sure you hear your child out fully before jumping in with your interpretation of the situation. Allowing your child to verbalise their concerns will help them better process and put meaning to what has happened.

5. **PROBLEM SOLVE WITH YOUR CHILD** Once you have identified your child's emotions and the situation that helped fuel them, as well as listened to your child's concerns so they feel understood, it's time to look at possible solutions. It's likely that your child will initially have no idea what their options are for handling their emotionally charged situation. Offer a few suggestions to get things rolling and then check with your child if these suggestions would work. If they wouldn't, ask them why. For example: 'So, we

both know that monsters aren't real, but you're still scared of them. Do you think blocking up under the bed with pillows would help you feel better?' The more questions you ask and the more your child feels a part of coming up with a solution, the more likely your child will be to act on making change. Even if you come up with the solution, as long as your child feels they have the ultimate say about whether to choose or reject the offered solution, it's more likely they'll take ownership and adopt it.

Incorporating these five points when around your child will help increase both of your emotional intelligence. If you are feeling unsure about your own ability to apply these five steps when talking to your child, you may want to reread this section of the book next time the situation arises. It won't be long before you notice how naturally these steps come to you. Practice is the key.

Summing up

IQ scores make up only part of a person's overall intelligence levels. Avoid the IQ trap by focusing on developing your child's emotional intelligence too. A person who is comfortable with, understands and can positively control their emotions is said to be high in emotional intelligence, and in a much stronger position to have a happy and fulfilled life. Teaching your child to understand their own emotions by being an emotion coach is one of the most precious gifts you can give them. Starting today, look for opportunities where you can use the five steps for helping foster your child's emotional intelligence.

24

PASS ON PASSING ON FEARS

'There is no sadder sight than a young pessimist.'

MARK TWAIN

It's natural to want to protect your child from harm. Unfortunately, this innate parental drive, if not handled properly, can cause negative outcomes for a child's confidence levels. When a parent tries to protect their child from a fear they themselves have, the parent risks passing on this fear to their child.

Mary was a mother of three young children. She came and saw me for counselling because she wanted to fix her phobia of spiders. While explaining her phobia to me, Mary joked that her mum also had a phobia of spiders and so did her grandmother. She said that when she was growing up, both her mother and grandmother would rush the children out of the room if there was a spider and not allow anyone back in until one of the men came and disposed of it. She suspected her phobia had been passed on from them, and now she didn't want to pass on the same phobia to her children.

All phobias are learned, usually by children watching a parent's reaction to certain things. Children take their cues as to what is dangerous in life from the adults closest to them. If your child sees you focusing on an object or situation in an unhealthy way, they will be more likely to focus on that object or situation in a similar fashion. Common types of fears that are passed on from parent to child include fears of:

* animals or insects
* stepping out of a comfort zone
* heights or confined spaces
* water, such as the beach, rivers and pools
* being alone at night-time (often the child is allowed to sleep in the parent's bed just as much for the parent's benefit)
* speaking in public
* becoming sick with any number of illnesses or diseases.

Many fears that are passed on to children can be so subtle that they go unnoticed by the parent. For example, when a child wants to try something new and their parent pulls a strange face when asked. This subtle body language can be enough to place doubt in the child's mind as to their own ability.

One classic psychology study demonstrated how easily a young child can pick up a fear from their primary caregiver. The study involved mothers and their twelve-month-old babies. Each mother was with her baby throughout the study, but the mothers were divided into two groups, A and B. Both groups A and B were exposed to the same situation, the only difference being that group B mothers had to positively encourage their baby to continue playing with the thing in front of them, whereas the mothers in group A just had to be themselves in response to what their baby was playing with. What were these babies playing with? An extremely large but tame python. The study went as follows: the children from group A were placed on the floor so the python could slither among them. As the fear of snakes is innate in humans but isn't activated until approximately the age of two, these babies saw the python as a large toy. As the group A babies started playing with the live python, they looked up to see what their mothers were doing. The mothers, who were told to be themselves, naturally looked horrified. Seeing the fear on their mothers' faces, the babies burst into tears. When it was group B's turn, as instructed the mothers laughed and encouraged their babies to keep playing with the python. As a result these babies were grabbing and chewing on the python, all because their mothers were supportive of their new toy. The study highlighted how a baby will first look to their parent's reaction in determining if a new situation is safe or not.

In the same vein, your child will be looking at your reaction when they are faced with a new challenge. How can you help prevent passing on unnecessary fears to your child? There are two important concepts to be mindful of:

1. Know your own fears

Sounds simple but many fears that we pass on to children can be so subtle that they go undetected. The mothers passing on their fear of the python was obvious; Mary's fear of spiders being passed on from her mother and grandmother was a little less obvious; though the parent who pulls a funny face upon hearing their child's intention to enter a public speaking competition at school could potentially go under the radar. In the last case, the parent was terrified of public speaking themselves, and the thought of their child being potentially humiliated triggered this fear, hence their response. By knowing your own fear, you are in a much better position to deal with it. This can be done by confronting it yourself, such as supporting your child in facing what you are scared of. Alternatively, if you feel your fear is too strong to face it alone, you could seek professional help from a psychologist.

2. Control your own reaction

The mothers in the python test controlled their own reactions to the situation, which determined how their babies would respond. Once you know *your* fear, focus on controlling your own reaction while encouraging your child to step out of a comfort zone. Even if this means faking your enthusiasm to hide your fear, do it. You may feel awful about your child wanting extra independence, like catching the school bus or waiting for you at the front school gate instead of in their classroom. But being supportive of your child stepping out of realistic comfort zones is a fundamental ingredient in developing their confidence.

Summing up

Fears are often passed on from parent to child for the child's safety. However, when the fear is unrealistic or prevents the child from developing, the parent's fear needs to be addressed. Know your own fears and confront them where possible. If this means hiding your fear from your child to encourage them to go forward, do it. If you can't control your fear alone, seek professional help.

25

LISTEN WITH YOUR EYES

*'The eyes have one
language everywhere.'*

GEORGE HERBERT

At birth, a baby's eye is about 75 per cent of the size of an adult eye. This is why babies look so cute – their big beautiful eyes are out of proportion to the size of their head. The eyes are a powerful aid in engaging with other people. But it takes courage to use one's eyes to advantage, which many shy adults weren't taught as children.

I recall my schoolteacher screaming at me, 'Look at me when I'm speaking to you.' She did this when she was correcting some form of my behaviour that she deemed inappropriate. At the time, all I could think was that it felt much safer staring down at my feet. I was fast learning to associate maintaining eye contact with threat.

Even though I couldn't have explained it at the time, I instinctively knew that staring at an angry adult was confrontational, a sign of wanting a fight. Years later, in the final years of high school, I had the opportunity to test out my theory. Right in the middle of a whole school assembly, a bullying teacher started screaming at me for talking. This time I took a different approach and, instead of looking at my feet, I calmly stared the teacher right in the eye as he attempted to berate me in public. His berating quickly stopped and I was sent to the principal's office for showing aggression towards a teacher. Children instinctively know that maintaining eye contact with an angry adult equals potential danger. When a child gets in trouble from an adult and is made to maintain eye contact, the child learns to associate it with something to avoid.

Shy adults suffer from an inability to maintain eye contact. Studies show that people unknowingly perceive others who can't maintain eye contact as untrustworthy, unconfident and unreliable. Those who *can* maintain eye contact are perceived as more trustworthy, confident and reliable. As many shy adults have told me, avoiding eye contact with others affects both their relationships and the types of jobs they can get. Developing your child's confidence to maintain eye contact could help in preventing shyness in later life.

How can you help foster your child's confidence to maintain eye contact when talking to other people, especially adults? An effective way is to make a game out of it.

The 'TV reporter' game

Pretend to be a TV reporter and interview your child about something good they have done. Use anything that resembles a fake microphone, like a hairbrush. It doesn't matter what the microphone is, just as long as there is something tangible for your child and you to talk into. The microphone acts as a prompt for whose turn it is to talk. As soon as you take the microphone away from your child, they'll instinctively know this means they can stop talking. This is good if they initially become shy or tongue-tied trying to find the right words to your questions. Make sure to start with questions your child can easily answer, like 'What's your favourite colour?', 'What's your favourite meal?' and 'What did you do at lunchtime today?'.

Once you have your microphone, explain to your child that it's important when being interviewed to maintain eye contact with you, the interviewer, as they will look more confident and professional on TV. Remember, you are trying to lower their natural association of danger with maintaining eye contact. So the more fun and crazy you can make the interview game, the easier it will be for your child to maintain eye contact.

Once you feel your child has mastered being interviewed and has maintained good eye contact, give them a go at interviewing you. By going first, you will have modelled how the interviewer maintains eye contact. It's even more important for the interviewer to maintain it than the interviewee, and it's the role of the interviewer that you ultimately want your child to master.

Encourage your child to interview other family members and, if possible, other adults your child feels comfortable with, such as a neighbour or aunt. Wise up the other adult beforehand as to what you're aiming to achieve from the interview. Suggest to the adult that they make a positive comment about your child maintaining eye contact.

If money permits, I strongly recommend purchasing a cheap recording device, either a sound recorder or a video camera, so your child can actually review the interviews. This takes the game to a whole new level of fun and gives them a reason to interview other people, as older children will be less likely to want to interview another adult using a hairbrush for a microphone.

Model maintaining eye contact

Another way to teach maintaining eye contact is to control your own actions when around your child. As we've seen in other chapters, children are always watching and learning from their parents' actions. So get to know the actions that you're modelling to your child in regards to maintaining eye contact. What is your eye contact like when talking to other adults? If it's an area you could improve in, make it your goal to do so by facing it gradually. Likewise, do you maintain eye contact when talking to your child? Often when a parent is engrossed in something and the child asks a question, the parent will try to ignore the child or give an answer without lifting their eyes. If you are too busy to talk, where possible, look at your child while you explain why you can't talk at the moment and give them a definite time when you will be able to. You may even consider letting your child know that you are working on maintaining eye contact when talking to others. This way they'll pay special attention when you model maintaining eye contact in social interactions. Being consistent with maintaining eye contact when speaking to anyone will help avoid sending mixed messages to your child.

Summing up

Maintaining eye contact gives the instant message to other people of confidence, trustworthiness and honesty. Encourage your child to maintain eye contact when talking to adults by making a game out of it. Likewise, be mindful of what messages you are sending your child about the way you maintain eye contact when speaking with others, including your child.

26

HONESTY HELPS PREVENT CONFUSION

'Avoid suspicion: when you're walking through your neighbour's melon patch, don't tie your shoe.'

CHINESE SAYING

It's natural for a parent to want to protect their child from harm. As a result, parents will often keep the truth from children in an attempt to protect them. Even though this can be necessary at times, the danger with hiding the truth from your child is that they are experts at reading you, and will know that something is not right. The child will then try to piece together what they think the issue is, which is where things can go horribly wrong. Because a child's brain is still developing, they don't have the ability to rationalise a situation like an adult. This forces them to try to make reason out of the unknown. The result? Children often blame themselves for their parents' emotional state.

Harrison's mum, Wendy, had been suffering from agonising pain for some years, ever since a routine medical operation that went horribly wrong, nearly killing her and leaving irreversible nerve damage. Some days Wendy's pain was so great that she had to muster up all her strength to hold back the tears. The reason Wendy didn't show her pain was that she didn't want Harrison to know how serious the problem really was. So she tried to do things that all the other mums at Harrison's school did, like helping with class reading groups. Even though Wendy hid her pain from him, Harrison wouldn't leave her side and became anxious when his mum was out of his sight. On a day when the pain was excruciating and Wendy had to use all her courage to appear normal, she was shocked when Harrison brought her some paracetamol and said, 'Here, Mum, this should help the pain.'

Even though Wendy and Harrison's situation is not common, Harrison's ability to read his mum is. At times parents can pull the wool over their child's eyes, such as pretending Santa Claus and the Easter Bunny are real. But this only sets parents up with a false sense of security that they can hide anything from their child. Children view the world through their parents. Seeing their parent's reaction first allows the child to determine if a situation is safe. This was evident with the experiment explained in chapter 24, where the children were playing with a live python. Make no mistake, your child is constantly watching you in an attempt to gauge the safety of their world.

When a child is raised in a situation of potential danger or uncertainty, their brains develop around looking for danger. As a result, the child becomes used to being on full alert. Unfortunately this is a classic way of decreasing a child's confidence. Confidence comes from a child knowing what to expect, and then having the self-efficacy that they can handle the challenge. Yet when a child is left guessing as to when the danger is coming, or what the actual danger is, it takes away their sense of control over their world.

Common confidence-lowering situations where a parent isn't honest with their child:

* an abusive household where excuses are made for the abusive parent's actions

* financial strain, where the parents try to hide it from the children

* not telling the child the truth about an ill parent, grandparent or family pet

* giving vague or ambiguous answers to a child's questions.

How can you help increase your child's confidence in response to the many and varied hardships in life? Start by honestly talking with your child about pressing issues instead of leaving it up to their imagination to solve. Wendy worked up the courage and explained to Harrison what her condition was and what it would and wouldn't let her do. He paused for some time and then told his mum that he felt responsible for her being sick because he wasn't at the hospital to protect her. After Harrison had the full story, his attitude started changing for the better and, even though Wendy's pain didn't subside, she found it more manageable because she didn't have to put precious energy into maintaining a front.

Often children are better able to cope than their parents think, once they know the full story. But what if it's inappropriate to go into detail with your child, such as finding out your partner has been unfaithful? In these cases, be honest with your child by letting them know that you and your partner are trying to sort out some problems, but that it is in no way their fault. Try to take out as much of the guesswork as possible for your child. Another example where it may not be appropriate to give all of the details is if the facts of the death of a friend or family member are very distressing. Leave out the details and simply explain that the person passed away due to a reason that is more child-friendly. Be warned, if you don't give some sort of explanation of how the person died, your child is likely to fill in the blanks themselves. Your child may develop the irrational belief that it was because the person was naughty, for instance, which results in a fear of death whenever someone does something naughty or wrong.

Your child will detect when there's something wrong by your reaction. So be honest with them about the situation, but tone down or replace the parts that are not suitable for your child's ears.

Commit to giving clear answers

Another important area to be honest with your child is in the responses you give to their questions. If you have ever been in a relationship where the other person won't commit, or had a boss who is vague in what they expected from you, you'll know how frustrating it can be not knowing where you stand. Ambiguous answers to a person's questions create a sense of confusion and self-doubt. Parents are often guilty of giving vague and ambiguous answers to their child's questions as a way of having control over the child or to get out of committing to anything. For example:

Child: 'Can we go to the park and play?'
Parent: 'We'll see.'

Child: 'Can I have a treat if I'm good at the shops?'
Parent: 'I'll think about it.'

Commit to giving clear answers to your child's questions, especially when you know it's an answer they won't want to hear, like the 'No' in advance of having a treat at the shops. If you are unable to make a decision at a particular point in time, let them know when you will come back to them with an answer. A confident child is one who knows where they stand. Empower your child by giving clear answers to their questions.

Honesty with discipline

The final area of honesty that needs mentioning is disciplining your child. Some parents can fall into the trap of telling a child lies to make them behave.

Brandy had trouble making her five-year-old daughter, Zara, wear a seatbelt in the car. After much frustration, she finally told her daughter that if she didn't put her seatbelt on, the police would come and take her away. To Brandy's surprise, it worked! From then on whenever Zara wouldn't put on her seatbelt, Brandy only had to ask the question, 'You don't want the police to take you away, do you?' and Zara would quickly put on her seatbelt. One day they were both at Zara's friend's house for a play, when the friend's dad called home from work to get something. He was a police officer, in uniform. Zara froze with fear and burst into tears, believing that the police had come to take her away. Brandy calmed her daughter down, and then later explained to the father why her daughter had been so terrified seeing him in uniform. The father jokingly said, 'I hate how parents use police as a scapegoat to discipline their child. It's a job you should be doing yourself.'

Have you not been totally honest in disciplining a child? The scapegoat doesn't have to be police; other common examples include saying:

* 'You'll get in trouble from the shop assistant if you climb up on the counter.'

* 'Santa won't bring you any presents if you're naughty.'

* 'If you keep misbehaving then Anthony will give you a smack.' (This actually happened at a carols by candlelight night, when my wife's friend said this to her rowdy son in an attempt to discipline him.)

* 'The orphanage will come and take you away if you keep misbehaving.'

These examples all highlight the same fact: the parent is either scared or doesn't know how to discipline their child, so needs to rely on lies and manipulation. A detailed look into how to discipline your child is beyond the scope of this book. However, the golden rule is to be loving, honest and consistent. Tell your child why they have to follow a rule and what punishment they will bring upon themselves if they choose not to follow it. Then be true to your word and deliver the punishment if your child chooses that path. For example, while in the home driveway, Brandy can say to her daughter, 'Zara, you need to wear a seatbelt for your own protection in case of an accident. If you don't put your seatbelt on by the time I count to three then we won't be going to your friend's house to play. What do you choose to do, Zara?' Now if she chooses not to put her seatbelt on, she also chooses not to go to her friend's house to play. This requires a parent to be strong and stand by their word. It only takes a few tries and children respond amazingly well to this technique of letting them choose their own outcome. By being honest and giving your child choices, it gives them a clearer understanding about consequences in life.

Summing up

A child knows when things aren't right with their parent. Yet their developing brains are not equipped to rationally solve problems like an adult can, so they often blame themselves for a parent's unhappiness. Whether it is discussing a pressing issue or giving clear answers to their questions, avoid suspicion by being honest with your child. When a child knows what to expect and feels they have the resources to cope, their confidence and self-efficacy to take on new challenges increase.

27

STICK TO THEIR SPEED LIMIT

'Why do they call it rush hour when nothing moves?'

ROBIN WILLIAMS

Thanks to time-saving devices like dishwashers, microwave ovens and washing machines, humans should have more spare time than ever before. But ironically we seem to have less because we work longer hours to pay for all these new time-saving gadgets and other luxuries. As a result of this rushed lifestyle, we have become obsessed with the number of hours in a day. In an attempt to help the overworked person save time, instant dinners, speed-cleaning, speed-reading, speed-dating and even speed-yoga are now becoming the norm for many.

The danger with leading such fast-paced, time-poor, stress-filled lives is that we can unintentionally transfer our obsession with time onto our children and push them to go at the same stressful speed. The barrage of music lessons, art lessons, dancing classes, sports, language studies, tutoring and completing homework and assignments, all while maintaining excellent school grades, causes children to be pushed at speeds that their bodies aren't yet ready for. Sadly, many experts suggest that high expectations, fast-paced living and preventing children from being children all lead to an increase in mental illness in young people. They simply can't keep up with the pressure placed on them.

Heath had a full life for an eleven-year-old. Each day after school he had something on. Mondays he had piano lessons, Tuesdays soccer training, Wednesdays swimming lessons. On Thursdays he had tutoring to improve his school grades followed by more soccer training, and Fridays were free with time allotted for piano practice for upcoming exams. Saturday mornings were devoted to competition soccer and Sundays to church with the family. School homework also had to fit in to this busy schedule. The only time Heath had time to himself was when he was asleep. Yet Heath's parents believed that pushing their son would provide him with the greatest chance of success in life.

Pushing your child to succeed can be a great thing. It can make children achieve more in life, give them a better education, and offer as many opportunities in life as possible. However, it has to be a balance: pushing a child too hard can be detrimental to both their physical and psychological wellbeing.

Children aren't adults and need to go at a pace suitable for a child. By pushing your child at adult speeds, you are exposing them to one of our number one killers: stress. Stress is fast becoming one of the biggest health issues in our society and has been shown to cause:

* digestive tract problems

* migraines

* high blood pressure

* skin conditions

* heart problems and strokes

* joint and muscle pain

* decreased memory and concentration

* anxiety and depression

* lowering of the immune system, and therefore an increase in colds and flu

* an addiction to adrenalin

* cancer

* sleeping problems, e.g. sleep walking, teeth grinding, sleep talking, nightmares, insomnia

* nervous twitches

* issues around eating too much or not enough

* abusing drugs and/or alcohol.

Even though this list is not exhaustive, the other danger with pushing your child too hard is the potential to negatively affect your relationship with them. Common causes include:

* **RESENTMENT** Children often begin to resent their parents for being so hard on them, feeling as if they can never be good enough.

* **OVERACHIEVING** A child who is pushed too hard can learn to associate achievement with gaining a parent's love. This sets a child up to feel they always have to do better, causing perfectionist and workaholic tendencies in later life.

* **ANGER** When a child is repeatedly pushed too hard or against their will by the parent, the child can become angry and rebel. This paves the way for potential risk-taking and deviant behaviour, such as using drugs or alcohol, shoplifting, vandalism, unsafe sex or self-harm.

Parents are often divided about whether to push their child or not. After all, research has shown both the consequences if children are pushed too hard and the consequences if children are not pushed hard enough, from being overprotected or, at the other end of the continuum, from being neglected. How can you as a parent navigate through the maze of knowing how hard to push your child? The answer is finding a balance.

Finding a balance

To find a balance, you don't look at what pace you can cope with, but rather what pace your child can. Let them determine their own speed limit by giving them space to be themselves. You can help achieve this in the following ways.

WATCH THEIR ENTHUSIASM LEVELS Generally, if your child is interested you will not be able to keep them away from the activity. So watch your child's enthusiasm levels regularly. Most elite performers, from the arts to sport and science, have had a deep love for what they do since they were young. Stories of athletes who continually practised their sport in the backyard, even when it was pitch-black, are common. When your child is engaged in their activity, does their body language suggest a keen interest? Or a lack of it? If there's a lack of interest and this has persisted for some weeks, it suggests that change of some description may be needed.

LISTEN TO YOUR CHILD Talk to your child and ask whether they are happy doing their activity, especially if their body language suggests otherwise. Likewise, if they could change their activity to something else, what would it be? If your child is unhappy, the question needs to be asked: Who is your child doing this activity for, themselves or you? For example, the child who hates playing football and much prefers tennis, but his father refuses as no son of his will play such a sissy game. It's crucial that you really look at your motivation behind your child doing the activities they do.

HAVE UNSTRUCTURED TIME It's important that a child have structured time, such as sport, dancing or music lessons, but it's just as important that they be allowed to have unstructured time too. If every moment of the day is planned out for them, they are robbed of the ability to entertain themselves, making them reliant on others. Have a set time each week where you can *make time to waste time*. Either play with your child and let them determine how the play will go or let them entertain themselves, preferably without TV or the computer.

Summing up

The right amount of pushing can lead your child to do great things, but too much can be harmful. Be sure that when you push your child you are doing it for the right reasons by involving your child's opinion as well. Avoid the negative impacts of pushing too hard by keeping your child's life balanced. Provide both structured and unstructured time so that your child has the best chance at a balanced and happy life.

28

HUGS, HORMONES AND HAPPINESS

*'The best gift you can give is a hug:
one size fits all and no one ever
minds if you return it.'*

ANONYMOUS

In the early 1900s, North American and European orphanages had an almost 100 per cent death rate of children under two years of age. These children were well looked after physically; they had all the food and health care they needed. Yet they died in their hundreds. Why? At the time no one was allowed to touch the children as it was thought that cuddling infants would spread infections and make them emotionally weak. The belief that you spoiled an infant by holding them or responding quickly to their cries was widely held. Then in the 1920s, Dr J. Brenneman, a hospital paediatrician, introduced a rule in his hospital that every baby should be picked up, carried around and mothered several times a day. Death rates fell dramatically. This paved the way for a revolution in the way children were raised.

Thankfully, parents are now encouraged to cuddle their children from birth. It's only recently, due to modern science, that we are discovering the physiological and psychological benefits of physical contact. Gentle physical touch from another person in a non-threatening way is the lifeblood for humans. If you have ever tried to massage yourself you'll know how difficult it is to get the same relaxing effects compared with someone else doing it for you. When we are hugged by another person, the brain releases feel-good hormones into the body called endorphins. These endorphins make us feel alive, increase self-esteem, improve brain function, lower stress, increase immune function and can even speed up the body's ability to repair itself from an injury.

However, even with all these benefits, research shows that the number of hugs a child receives from birth decreases with age, and drops even more radically if the child is a boy. This isn't always the fault of the parent. Children often resist hugs as they get older.

Hug for no reason

Often parents forget to hug their child not because they are bad parents, but because they are distracted by trying simply to survive in a fast-paced life. What can you do to increase your child's daily intake of hugs? Start by making it a rule that you give your child a hug at the start and end of each day, for instance when they leave for school and when they go to bed. Associate giving your child hugs with teeth brushing; you brush your teeth both at the start and at the end of the day. This simple practice of giving regular hugs will help increase your child's sense of inner security.

Once you have this two-hugs-a-day baseline to work from, hug your child for no other reason than because you can. If a child learns to associate hugs solely with achieving good school grades or succeeding at music, art or sport, they're learning that your love is conditional on whether they are successful.

Hug when angry

Hugs can unintentionally indicate to a child conditional love. This is because in our society, hugs are generally seen as a reward. Rarely do we go up and hug someone who has annoyed us, especially our children. However, children need hugs when they deserve them the least. Naturally, discipline your child if they have done wrong. But once you have disciplined them and they know why they were punished, hug them. Some people cringe at this, believing that a child will learn to associate getting hugs with being naughty. If the only time you hug your child is after they are naughty, then this would be true. But if you hug your child at other times, and for no reason, they won't make this association.

What if your child doesn't like to be hugged?

What if your child doesn't like hugs or won't allow you to hug or touch them for long? This is more common the older a child gets. Often it's not seen as cool to be hugged by a parent. How do you get around this problem? Tickle! Science shows that it's impossible for a person to tickle themselves. A quick way of releasing feel-good endorphins in your child is to tickle them. The advantage with tickling is that it's great for bonding and doesn't take long. What's more, being tickled has been shown to be an aerobic workout, which is why a child is often exhausted after a good tickle. Then you can capitalise on their exhaustion by finishing off with a hug.

Other ways of making physical contact without hugs:

* do their hair (generally better suited to girls)

* give a high five

* massage their shoulders or feet (yes, feet sounds awful, but it slips past their guard)

* give them a back scratch

* give a bear hug or wrestle (playfully)

* give a pat on the back

Summing up

Physical contact, especially through hugs and tickles, is a great way of boosting your child's physical and mental wellbeing. Hug your child daily, especially during times they deserve it least. That way your hugs will indicate to your child that your love for them is unconditional and not dependent on their achievements. If your child is a little more hesitant to let you hug them, be creative. Remember, the goal is to make regular physical contact with your child in a non-threatening way. A hugged child is a happy child.

29

CONFIDENT KIDS TALK TO THEMSELVES

'The world we have created is a product of our thinking. It cannot be changed without changing our thinking.'

ALBERT EINSTEIN

Many people would be nervous to admit that they talk to themselves, even though it is a normal thing to do. Psychologists estimate that when we talk to ourselves, which is known as self-talk, we do so at more than 500 words per minute, with the majority of it negative. As thoughts often trigger the way we feel and behave, most people are unsuspectingly at the mercy of their negative thinking.

If very few adults are even aware of how they talk to themselves, it's little wonder that children are totally in the dark when it comes to knowing their self-talk.

Ben was a real worrywart. His worries weren't about one specific thing, but jumped from one issue to another. He worried that the house would burn down while he and his family were inside asleep, that his teacher wouldn't like his homework, that his mum would have a car accident on the way home from work, and that his friends at school would no longer like him. Ben's parents tried ignoring his worries, but this only made them worse. They started modifying their own lives around Ben's worries: they installed a special lock on Ben's bedroom window to keep out burglars; his mum phoned the school to say she'd got to work safely; they left all household appliances unplugged when not in use; and they avoided eating fish with bones, in case someone choked on them. However, for every worry his parents diffused, a new one would quickly take its place. Eventually Ben's parents resigned themselves to having to constantly reassure their son and cater to his worries.

Chronic worriers like Ben have a condition known as Generalised Anxiety Disorder, which is fuelled by negative self-talk. Even if your child is not a worrier like Ben, they'll still have moments in their life where they'll be affected by worry. How would you know if your child's worry is a problem? There are three common things to look for:

* Your child's worry won't go away no matter how much they are reassured.

* Their worries have grown worse with time.

* The worry starts showing in other parts of their lives, e.g. they won't go to their friend's house in case the house burns down.

Generally, all children worry. It's the degree that differs. Even if your child's worries are not like Ben's, it's still of use to teach how to manage them. You do this by teaching your child how to talk to themselves. Children are taught how to add numbers, spell words and even know how the stars and planets operate. Rarely are they taught how to recognise and control their own thoughts. With so many young people suffering from mental health problems, schools are taking more interest in this vital area. Some of the benefits of teaching your child to control their self-talk include:

* being able to pick themselves up when feeling unhappy

* having more control over their moods

* feeling more confident to step out of comfort zones and try new things

* understanding the connection between their thoughts, feelings and actions.

If getting to know one's self-talk is so important, how can you teach your child to get to know theirs?

Use yourself as a 'self-talk' role model

Teach your child to become aware of their own self-talk by using yourself as a role model. Make it a game that your child has to guess what your self-talk is in relation to your body language. For example, get your child to determine what your self-talk is when you're pretending to be happy after making a successful shot in basketball. Having your child help you identify your own self-talk will teach them to spot their own. Here are some other types of body-language situations you can pretend to display in order to help identify your self-talk:

* Look sad after pretending to break something precious. *Self-talk:* I'm always making mistakes.

* Look happy wondering what's in the gift you're about to unwrap. *Self-talk:* This is exciting, I wonder what it could be.

* Look scared because you see a big dog while walking to school. *Self-talk:* The dog will bite me.

* Look shy about speaking to an adult. *Self-talk:* I don't know what to say.

It's here that you can act out current fears that your child may be experiencing. At first you may have to prompt them as to what your self-talk is, but after a few goes they will get the hang of it. Identifying self-talk is the first and often most difficult step. Once self-talk has been identified, you can get to work on changing it.

Detective thinking

Children love being detectives and looking for clues. Teach them to act like a detective and look for evidence to see if their unhelpful self-talk is really correct. If the self-talk is that there's a large monster in their bedroom cupboard, test it by determining if a large monster could really fit in there. Has there ever been a monster in there before? If not, why would it start now? Do large monsters really exist? If so, prove it. For adults, detective thinking may sound basic and nearly too simple to work, but research shows that children take to this form of problem solving amazingly well as it gives them understanding about their environment.

Spotting the problem

If your child appears worried, what is the best way to help them spot their unhelpful self-talk? Use the following three strategies, in order:

1. Listen to your child without trying to give answers so you get the full story and understand what their unhelpful self-talk is.

2. Once you have got the full story, reassure your child by helping them correct any misconceptions or unhelpful self-talk they may have by using detective thinking.

3. Finally, encourage and support your child to use their new self-talk to face the situation that scares them, e.g. monitor their self-talk while practising a school speech at home.

Summing up

Identifying and then controlling one's self-talk is potentially one of the most important things a person can do to help ensure good mental health. This simple process is an invaluable skill for your child to learn. A child who can control what they tell themselves is a child who is in better control of both their happiness and confidence levels.

30

ENCOURAGE MISTAKES

'The greatest mistake you can make in life is to be continually fearing you will make one.'

ELBERT HUBBARD

Why is it that when we become fixated on not making a certain mistake, we often end up making it? When the mind becomes so focused on what it doesn't want, it loses track of what it does want. As a result, the mistake you want to avoid ironically becomes the goal for the mind to achieve. Trying to avoid mistakes can be one of the greatest hindrances to originality and success. If you encourage your child to make mistakes, it becomes a form of reverse psychology and actually frees them up to try new things. Making mistakes is the way we humans, especially children, learn best.

One study, conducted by Stanford University, explored whether being praised for making mistakes had a difference on children's choices. Four hundred fifth graders were given a test to complete. Regardless of their scores, half the children were randomly and briefly praised as being 'really smart' for doing well on the test, while the other half were praised solely for 'trying hard'. Then the children were given two tasks that they could choose from: one task was easy and they'd learn little but do well; the other task was more challenging and interesting but would produce more mistakes. The majority of the children praised for being smart on the initial test chose the simple task, while 90 per cent of those praised solely for trying hard chose the more difficult task. The researchers were surprised that when the children were briefly praised for being smart they were then less likely to take on a more challenging task, whereas the children who were briefly praised for trying hard were more likely.

The study gives food for thought as to the impact the type of praise given to children has on their willingness to try new things. However, this willingness to try new things is compromised by the mixed messages we give about making mistakes. On the one hand, children are taught that everyone makes mistakes and that the great thinkers embraced the mistake-making process. A quote from Thomas Edison, who tried thousands of times before successfully inventing the light bulb, is often used in schools: 'I have not failed. I have just found ten thousand ways that won't work.' But on the other hand, children are also taught that mistakes are bad and should be avoided. Good exam results are rewarded for getting things right, not for making errors; losing athletes aren't rewarded with a big trophy; and compliments are often awarded for giving the correct answer in class, whereas the wrong one may make the other students laugh. The result? Children grow up thinking that making mistakes is a necessary learning tool but should still be avoided.

As adults, we unwittingly model to our children the importance of avoiding mistakes and reinforce the importance of always being right. Often when we get things wrong we either beat ourselves up mentally, blame someone else or try to cover it up. What we avoid doing is learning from our mistakes. Because of this tendency to steer clear of mistakes, we create a perfect image of ourselves to our children. Even though this might feed a parent's ego, it won't help the child feel comfortable in making mistakes. What you need to do is take yourself off the pedestal that your child has made for you by creating a 'mistake-safe' environment at home.

To teach your child to feel safe making mistakes you need to follow two steps:

1) Lead by example and show your child how to make mistakes.

2) Praise your child when they make a mistake trying something new.

Step 1: Lead by making mistakes yourself

Children naturally put their parents up on a pedestal, which feeds the belief that some people don't make mistakes. Most adults can attest to feeling crushed as a child when they learned the harsh truth that their parents were far from perfect. Help prepare your child for reality by sharing some of your comfort zones you're scared to step out of. This could be trying and failing something new, such as cooking something you haven't cooked before, riding a bicycle for exercise, doing further study, joining the gym or researching your family tree. Even though pride may make you reluctant to share your feared comfort zones, doing so will help your child to be less critical of themselves when they make mistakes.

As children naturally copycat their parents, you need to model making mistakes in front of them. The trick here is to be okay with making mistakes yourself instead of getting annoyed. This does take a bit of practice, because for many adults we have learned to avoid making mistakes. Turning mistake-making into a game and laughing at your mistakes will make the process feel much easier. Ways you can model making mistakes in front of your child:

* Cooking something new or adding a different ingredient and being okay with whatever it tastes like.

* Ordering a different food/drink/ice-cream from what you would normally order and putting it down to a learning experience, no matter how it tastes.

* Doing an activity with your child that you wouldn't normally do, e.g. rollerblading, riding a bike, going to a child-friendly concert.

* Drawing a picture of your child, especially if you aren't a natural artist, and then showing your child.

Remember, there will be a natural tendency to want to cover or justify your mistakes in front of your child. Resist the urge. Instead ask your child what you yourself could have learned from your mistakes. Be warned, if your child puts you down for your mistakes, such as saying you need to give up painting, this will be instant feedback on their beliefs about making mistakes. If this happens, be calm and explain to your child that it's okay to make mistakes. Remember, it's the way you handle yourself after making a mistake that they'll be watching and learning from the most.

Step 2: Praise your child when they make a mistake

As you are making mistakes by trying something new, encourage your child to join you. Emphasise the importance of 'trying hard' instead of 'trying to be right'. Then when your child does make a mistake while trying something new, praise them for trying.

In a similar way, have a rewards system for when your child tries something new. Simone was nervous to answer questions in class for fear of getting them wrong. Her mum made a deal with her: if she attempted to answer a question in class, regardless of whether it was right or wrong, they'd go and get an ice-cream together to celebrate. Simone's mum explained to her that this was based on honesty and that she trusted Simone to tell her the truth. A few days passed and Simone came home with a grin from ear to ear. 'I tried to spell a word in class and got it wrong, and the teacher said it was a good try.' Even though inconvenient at the time, Simone's mum stopped what she was doing, praised Simone for giving it a try and for being honest, and they both went down to the shop for an ice-cream.

In a similar way, if your child comes home dejected for trying something new at school and getting it wrong, use a bit of reverse psychology instead of just trying to comfort them – praise them. Take them out and celebrate as Simone's mum did. This is sure to make your child re-evaluate their belief system around making mistakes.

Summing up

Children learn most from making mistakes, but we as adults inadvertently encourage them not to make them. Encourage your child to make mistakes by transforming the home into a *mistake-safe* environment. Lead by example and show your child that it's safe to make mistakes when trying something new. Then praise your child for trying hard when they themselves make a mistake when trying something new. Confident kids make mistakes because they know both that it's okay to make them and that they provide valuable learning. The message you want to be sending to your child is not 'Be perfect' but 'We love it when you try, and when you learn by making mistakes.' What's something new that you and your child can make mistakes trying?

31

ORDER ICE-CREAM DECISIVELY

'My advice to you is not to inquire why or whither, but just enjoy the ice-cream while it's on your plate.'

THORNTON WILDER

Indecision can be crippling, keeping people in situations they don't like, such as jobs, relationships, housing or neighbourhoods. For children, indecision can be just as paralysing, preventing them from making new friends, trying new games or activities and even eating new types of food. Decision-making can trigger high emotion.

When fear of making the wrong choice comes into the decision-making process, it can be debilitating. If you have ever been stuck trying to choose between two things, such as whether to order a restaurant's special or the standard meal you've already had, you'll know how painful it can be. The fear of making a wrong choice often wins out, so we stick with the boring dish we've had countless times before. In this case, the predictable meal becomes a comfort food because we know what emotions it will trigger in us. Sticking with the comfort food means that we don't have to deal with the fear of making a wrong decision.

What's the problem with sticking with comfort foods instead of trying new ones? The way we handle ourselves with seemingly trivial issues like what food to order is often a blueprint for how we handle bigger issues in life. By sticking with comfort foods you are unconsciously teaching your child to avoid making decisions – that no decision is better than the wrong decision. The previous chapter showed that trying to avoid making mistakes around your child is a recipe for disaster as it only lowers their self-confidence. How then can you give your child the courage to step out of a comfort zone and risk making mistakes? You can start small, by teaching them that when it comes to ordering food, it is better to make a decision than no decision at all.

Start with a situation that is pleasant and doesn't involve a lot of pressure, like buying an ice-cream. Sounds easy, right? Here is the catch: you both have to choose an ice-cream that you have never eaten before, thereby avoiding the no-decision comfort food. Plus, you both have to choose your ice-cream within thirty seconds. Let your child know before entering the shop that there's only one rule: if they can't decide on a new flavour within the thirty seconds, you both leave the shop empty-handed. Sticking to the time limit may seem harsh, but it teaches your child two important things: to have faith in themselves to make the right decision and that *no decision* is often worse than the *wrong decision*.

No matter what flavour your child chooses, congratulate them on making such a fast decision. Remember, the goal is to make a fast decision, not the right decision. If this is not stressed to your child, they may beat themselves up mentally for not choosing an ice-cream that was as tasty as their favourite.

In a less time-limited version of the above exercise, go to a café with your child and order something from the menu other than your usual. It doesn't matter whether it is food or drink, just as long as you have not had it before. Let your child know in advance what you're doing and encourage them to also step out of a comfort zone and try a new food or drink. Make a game out of it; that way you'll both be motivating each other to step out of comfort zones.

The aim of these two exercises is to teach both of you to trust your abilities to make a fast decision without getting bogged down in fear. Often when you make a decision to be spontaneous and do something out of the ordinary, it makes you feel alive and free.

Summing up

Comfort food is comfortable because there are no surprises about the emotions it will elicit, but also because it doesn't require a decision. But comfort foods keep us from trying new experiences. Get to know your comfort foods. Then, in front of your child, model choosing and then eating or drinking something that you normally wouldn't try. It's important to make this spontaneous decision-making fun. This will help reduce your child's fear of making a wrong decision by teaching them not only that life doesn't always have to be serious but also that not every decision has to be correct – a vital key in building a child's self-confidence. What comfort food can you and your child start on first?

32

MONOPOLISE YOUR CHILD

'I'd like to live as a poor man with lots of money.'

PABLO PICASSO

Research shows that people who become millionaires by winning the lottery are most likely to lose it quickly and become more depressed than before they won. On the other hand, many self-made millionaires have lost and regained their fortune at least once in their lives. Why is it that certain people are able to hold on to their money and make it grow, but others can't seem to hold on to it for long at all? Researchers claim that this is generally due to a person's beliefs about money, beliefs often unknown to the person themselves. It's vital that you become aware of the money beliefs you are passing on to your child, and determine whether these beliefs will help or harm their future.

Growing up, money was pretty scarce in our family, so I developed a great money-making trick, similar to capitalising on the goose that laid golden eggs. In my case it wasn't a goose but homing pigeons. Homing pigeons are renowned for their ability to fly away and then find their way back to where they regard home. The trick is that the caged pigeon needs to be kept in the same spot for a few weeks before it's conditioned to consider a place home. I would sell the birds to customers who knew nothing about homing pigeons. When they bought one, I would tell them that the homing pigeon only needed to be housed at their home for two days before it could be let go. Naturally, the pigeon would fly back to my place, where I would sell it again. This process allowed me to sell the same pigeons over and over.

Reflecting on my dishonest escapade, I can't say I'm proud. It actually makes me cringe thinking about it. The reason for telling you this story is to illustrate how parents' beliefs about money can be passed on so easily to children. This is not to say that my parents taught me to sell and resell pigeons. When I told them what I had done years later, they were horrified. But as a child I knew my parents were doing it tough financially, and they tried to keep it from us by avoiding our questions. While they were trying to protect their children, my parents were withholding information from us. This lack of honesty led me to make the connection that it was okay to be dishonest where money was concerned. Remember, as a child's brain is still developing, they are forced to put their own meaning on things they don't understand.

We all have different beliefs about money. Some people believe money is evil, others worship it, and others still are indifferent. Generally a person's beliefs about money are influenced heavily by life experiences, especially as a child. These beliefs are rarely questioned and are instead taken as truth. Here is a short list of commonly held but opposing beliefs people may have about money:

* Money is the root of all evil *versus* Money is a tool that can be used for good.

* Invest today to enjoy tomorrow *versus* Enjoy today as there might not be a tomorrow.

* You should be able to have the finer things in life, even if it means going into debt *versus* Live within your means.

What are good money beliefs? The answer depends largely on your spiritual and ethical beliefs, which are both beyond the scope of this book. The purpose of addressing money beliefs is not to push a certain ideology – I've met both unhappy wealthy people and happy people with little – but it is to help you look honestly at your own beliefs, which you are passing on to your child. Once beliefs are looked at in the cold hard light of day, you can better assess their usefulness, and ultimately if they are of benefit to you and your child.

How can your money beliefs be passed down to your child? Simply in the way you act towards money. Here are some examples to help you think about the money beliefs your child is adopting:

* Is money in your home treated as a good or bad thing?

* Are family money issues discussed with your child or hidden from them?

* Does your child have an appreciation for money or do they believe money grows on trees (or in ATMs)?

* Is your child encouraged to save or spend?

* What degree of honesty and integrity, versus ruthlessness or dishonesty, does your child hold towards obtaining money?

* Is your child stingy or generous with money? If they are generous, is it by donating to others less fortunate or by giving it to their peers in an attempt to buy friends?

The purpose of this exercise is not to determine which beliefs are right and wrong, but to start making you aware of your child's money beliefs. A great way to uncover your child's hidden money beliefs is to play a board game like Monopoly with them. Not only will the game highlight your child's money beliefs but it will also show the beliefs you are passing on to your child. Keep the six points above in mind as you play so you become aware of money beliefs in your family. It may take a few games, but once these money beliefs are identified, you can reinforce the helpful ones and try correcting the unhelpful ones. Remember, lead by example. If you identify an unhelpful money belief in yourself, highlight this to your child and then show them how you could correct it.

A final note, if you are experiencing difficulties financially, consider talking to your child about it instead of trying to hide it from them. You don't necessarily have to go into detail, but let them know that money is tight at the moment. Children naturally want to help because their family is their life. Being able to help makes a child feel like a valued contributor in the family. Allow them to help solve the family financial problem in areas that are within their control. For example, your child may suggest to borrow their books or DVDs from the library instead of buying them, go without a holiday at the end of the year or have a more modest one, or even wear pre-loved clothing. Not only can children often handle honesty better than parents believe, but they also thrive if allowed to be part of the solution.

Summing up

Beliefs around money are as varied and diverse as the people who hold them. Get to know your own money beliefs so that you know what you are passing on to your child. Once you have established both your and your child's money beliefs, keep what is helpful and replace what isn't. Above all else, be honest with your child about money and, where possible, don't keep secrets from them about the state of the family finances. Starting today, how can you approach the topic of money with your child?

33

PICK YOUR FIGHTS

'In matters of principle, stand like a rock; in matters of taste, swim with the current.'

THOMAS JEFFERSON

Children have very little control or choice in their lives. Adults choose their clothes, food, toys and often even friends. When a child then wants to assert their independence and make their own choices, it can cause friction between parent and child.

Karl was a typical eight-year-old boy. He did what he was told but at times could be very strong-willed if it was something he felt passionate about. Karl's family were all going to watch his sister perform in her school concert and

Karl's mum had chosen a gorgeous blue button-up shirt for him to wear. But Karl protested, pleading that he wanted to wear the new T-shirt his parents had given him, one with his favourite rock band across the front. Even though the T-shirt wasn't offensive and Karl's mum quietly didn't have a problem with him wearing it, she was concerned about what her parents and others at the school would think. So she stood firm and said no. Karl also dug his heels in and refused to go to the concert if he had to wear a button-up shirt. The conflict was threatening to take the shine off the evening.

What would you do if you were in Karl's mother's shoes? Whether to give in to a child's requests is always a difficult issue for most parents. Your child might want to wear clothing that clashes, stay overnight at a friend's house, go to an under-18s disco, stay up late, watch certain TV shows or eat breakfast cereal for afternoon tea – finding the balance between standing your ground and giving in is never easy. Parents often want to develop their child's independence but feel that there's a risk it could:

* compromise their safety

* engender a lack of respect for authority

* make them spoilt and expect everything to go their own way.

How can you know when to stand your ground and when to give in to your child? As Thomas Jefferson so eloquently described it in his quote at the start of this chapter, you need only stand your ground on *matters of principle*, and let your child win the battle over *matters of taste*. It's easy for a parent to lump all arguments in the matters of principle category so that they can win every argument, but parenting isn't always that cut and dried, much to our egos' disappointment. At the end of the day, all arguments, even those with your child, are just two people's differing opinions of what is right and wrong. A good way to understand when your ego is being threatened, as opposed to your child's welfare, is to ask yourself a very simple question: Do I have to win this fight? If you can't imagine that letting your child win a particular fight will negatively affect themselves or anyone else, it's often a sure sign your ego is trying to protect itself by being right.

Here is a short list of different examples for each of the two categories:

Matters of principle	Matters of taste
Not allowing your child to stay at someone's house that you know very little about.	Permitting posters on your child's bedroom walls.

Matters of principle	Matters of taste
Watching a movie that you feel is inappropriate.	Letting them choose their own hairstyle (within reason).
Swimming unsupervised in a river or lake.	Using inoffensive popular slang terms that aren't correct English.
Walking home from an event at night.	Keeping their room tidy.

Compromise when saying NO

If it is a matter of principle and you say no to your child's request for their safety or welfare, then your word should be final. For situations where safety isn't an issue it's often worth considering a compromise after you've said no. By compromising you are giving your child a sense of control by meeting them halfway. For example, Karl's mother could suggest that he wear his band T-shirt underneath his shirt, and then remove his shirt at the end of the concert. This way Karl could show off his new T-shirt to his friends while still respecting both his grandparents and other adults who may take offence. If your child doesn't like your suggested compromise, it's their choice not to accept it.

Every parent's situation will be different, and I can't advise you in the space of one chapter what to do for all arguments with your child. But if you can take a moment to consider whether the argument is over principles or taste, it will help guide you to make a better decision. I've found that asking myself if I have to win the fight usually highlights whether I'm arguing with my child over principles or taste.

Summing up

Children have very little control over their lives. Let your child gain a sense of control over theirs where possible by picking your fights with them. Parents don't have to win every fight. Letting your child win the less important fights occasionally will return their sense of control. Are you arguing with your child over matters of principle or taste?

34

ALLOW YOUR CHILD TO FEEL PAIN

'Pain is inevitable, but suffering
is optional.'

UNKNOWN

We often feel uncomfortable seeing others experience pain
or discomfort. In an attempt to deal with this discomfort
we can respond negatively either by overreacting and
creating a drama or by under-reacting with the cold 'get
over it' approach.

It was Billy's birthday party and many of his friends and
some of the parents were visiting. While playing chasey,
Billy fell over and grazed his knees. Upon seeing her son's
injury, Billy's mother became distraught and raced him

inside to apply the necessary antiseptics and bandaids. He wasn't allowed to run for the rest of the day in case he injured himself further. Later in the party, Mikey fell off the trampoline and split his lip open. Upon seeing her son's injury, Mikey's mum coldly told him to stop crying and have some fun.

The mothers showed two totally different responses to their children's pain: Billy's mum overreacted by dramatising the situation; Mikey's mum under-reacted by neglecting her son's needs. Research has shown that both the under-reacting and overreacting approaches negate a child's ability to manage pain and discomfort. Let's have a look at these two unhelpful parenting methods in more detail to see why this is so.

Overreactors

It's likely you will know someone like Billy's mum, the worrywart, who is prone to creating mountains out of molehills. The overreacting approach works from a 'what if' perspective, so in Billy's mum's case, 'What if my child's pain is a sign of worse to come?' This style of parenting, where the person goes into hysterics and dramatises the situation after a child has been hurt, unconsciously increases the child's anxiety levels. Remember, children look to their parents to gauge whether a situation is safe. If the parent looks like they can't cope, they are unknowingly sending the child a message that they too won't be able to cope with the situation. This is a dangerously effective way of lowering a child's self-confidence in handling stress-provoking situations in the future.

Under-reactors

The stoic stiff-upper-lip approach that Mike's mum used is commonly promoted for dealing with not only emotional pain but also physical pain. The central tenet that this approach works from is that if you give a child's pain too much recognition, they'll become a hypochondriac. The major problem with going to the opposite end of the scale and under-reacting is that it gives a child the unconscious message that their pain is not warranted. This can be confusing for them because the child learns that their body's natural danger alarms are wrong and must therefore be ignored. A child in this case is being conditioned to be a bad patient as an adult, for example, leaving symptoms undiagnosed until a life-threatening illness crops up.

Solution

If your child genuinely hurts themselves, and you should neither dramatise the situation nor try to cover up your child's pain, what is the answer? Simple: just acknowledge their pain. Not acknowledging your child's pain communicates to them that they don't understand their emotions and they have it wrong. Likewise, overreacting teaches them that the situation is more catastrophic than it really is. Gently and calmly acknowledging your child's pain achieves two things: 1) It lets your child know that the physical symptoms their body is communicating are accurate; and 2) You believe in their ability to be able to cope with the situation and that it's not the end of the world.

Now you may be thinking this all sounds good in theory, but how do you calmly acknowledge your child's pain when a voice in your head is screaming either that the injury could be worse than it appears or that you'll make them soft? The way to stay balanced in response to your child's pain is to remain in control of your reaction. Do this by:

* talking in a calm and gentle voice

* acknowledging and confirming what they are feeling, e.g. 'Yes, that's normal for your grazed arm to be hurting.'

* asking them if they think they'll be okay, e.g. 'I think you'll be okay, what do you think?'

Often, when it's left up to your child, they'll quickly determine whether their response is excessive or not, based on your reaction. If you can focus on controlling your own reaction to the situation and display both concern and a sense of hope, this will have a positive effect on your child's reaction.

Practising the right response

The problem with practising this skill is that it requires your child to be injured, which is something no parent wants. So how can you safely refine your response to a potential injury, and foster your child's belief that they can cope, without your child having to be hurt? A great way is to watch a TV show where a person or cartoon character has been injured (preferably nothing graphic) and to ask your child if the person's response to the injury was warranted. Be aware of how you respond to the scene and the way you communicate, and also your child's answers. Their response will give you an idea of their beliefs around managing pain. If you identify either overreacting or under-reacting beliefs towards pain in their responses, you can gently correct them. If overreacting, reassure your child of your belief in them to cope. If under-reacting, let your child know that it's both normal and okay to feel pain. We fathers can often be guilty of under-reacting to our child's pain by trying to play it down.

Summing up

We all feel pain; it's our response to it which determines our ability to cope. When a parent either over- or under-reacts to their child's injuries, unhealthy beliefs around pain and discomfort can be fostered. Empathetically and calmly responding to your child's pain, and normalising what they are feeling, will help give them a sense of security and a belief that they can cope.

35

HAVE HOME CONCERTS

'Don't lower your expectations to meet your performance. Raise your level of performance to meet your expectations.'

UNKNOWN

Kristy said she felt sick on the day she was meant to give a speech in class. Her mother was aware of the speech so went along with Kristy's supposed sickness, because she, too, feared speaking in public. The thought of her daughter getting up in front of the class and being humiliated sent chills down her spine. There was an unwritten law in Kristy's family: never bring unnecessary attention to yourself that could result in embarrassment. This meant that things like having a photo taken, being filmed or playing charades weren't common in the family home.

Kristy and her family aren't alone in fearing public speaking. If our number one fear is rejection by others, then potentially the best representation of this is public speaking. Research shows that people fear performing in front of others, an off-shoot of the fear of rejection, more than dying.

Because of the innate fear associated with performing in front of other people, children need to be in an environment where they feel safe so that they can develop their performance skills. If a child doesn't have this environment, they will be more likely to be over-anxious and avoid performance-type situations in later life, such as public speaking, job interviews, dealing with authority figures, dating and careers that involve interaction with others. On the other hand, if a child has the opportunity to perform but the environment is judgemental, critical or unsafe, this too will be potentially harmful for their self-confidence.

The ability to perform in front of others is not limited to the arts. As Shakespeare once said, 'All the world's a stage.' Giving a presentation at work, being on the committee of a local group, making a speech at a special occasion, asking the boss for holidays or time off work and phoning a talkback radio station are all examples of performing. If you can help your child develop a belief in their own ability to perform in front of others and master this social fear, they will have a distinct advantage over others in the future.

How can you help your child develop their social performance skills? Encourage your child to put on a concert at home in front of you. Designate a stage area where they can perform, such as in front of the TV (make sure it's turned off). This will also provide a natural seating area on the lounge for the audience, namely you and other family members. Treat it as a real concert, introducing your child before they come on stage and applauding them when they do.

Possible ideas for a home concert:

* playing an instrument

* reading a story aloud

* telling a joke

* playing charades

* doing a dance

* doing karaoke or miming to a song

* being filmed on a video camera and then watching it back with the family (this can be good for the shy child as they'll still feel like they are performing when watching themselves on TV).

Remember, you need your child to feel that the home is a safe environment where they can practise their social performance skills. If this safety is not already established, asking your child to perform in front of you and the family will be like asking them to perform in front of thousands of people. Therefore, make sure criticism is kept to a minimum and go heavy on the praise, especially if your child is anxious about performing.

What if your child is too shy to perform?

If your child is reserved, you will have to approach this fear gradually and without pressure. In this case, the first step is teaching your child that the home is a safe environment for concerts. Make it a rule that when your child performs, under no circumstances is any criticism to be given, only praise. If your child starts to perform, say by playing charades, but then freezes from anxiety, praise them for getting up. Then hop up yourself and model to your child how it is done. Make sure you appear to be having fun when you do it by being silly, and avoid being serious or competitive. Be patient – little by little you'll be teaching your child that their home is safe, and in this way they can take a slightly bigger step with each new performance. Using the charades as an example, the next time your child has a turn, make their challenge simple to build their confidence. For instance, ask your child to write a letter in the air with their finger so you have to guess it. Then, when you guess it, praise your child. This is a safe way to give them a win and build confidence.

As your child feels more comfortable with performing in the family concerts, they will naturally take more risks by trying new things. Their performances might seem loud and silly, but let them go; they are experimenting with new social skills. If they get out of hand, stop the game until they calm down. Even though it's important that the concerts are safe, criticism-free zones, it's just as important that your child has clear limits of what is acceptable and unacceptable behaviour. Likewise, if it gets to the stage where your child wants to perform in public at every opportunity, calmly and gently let them know that social performances are only for certain situations. Brainstorm with your child where these appropriate situations might be. By teaching your child these types of limits they will learn what is and isn't socially acceptable. Being able to read an audience is an essential ingredient for any good performer.

Summing up

Whether it's entertaining a crowd, asking a question in class or chairing a meeting, to be a successful performer on any of life's stages, a person needs to have confidence in their own performance ability. Children have a natural drive to perform in front of others, which will only be hampered if the environment in which they are performing is not safe. Providing a safe environment at home where your child can practise their social performance skills can foster this vital skill. The child who has the confidence to perform in front of others has a huge advantage in life. Make the commitment to develop your child's performance skills by having family concerts.

36

ACT LIKE A BIRD

'Don't handicap your children by
making their lives easy.'

ROBERT A. HEINLEIN

Being called a 'bird brain' should no longer be an insult.
Scientists have discovered that a bird's brain is far more
advanced than we give them credit for. Birds from the corvid
family, such as crows, ravens and magpies, have recently
amazed scientists with astonishing feats of memory, an
ability for complex social reasoning and a gift for crafting
and using tools, all previously unseen in animals without
prior training. On top of this, we can also learn from birds'
parenting skills. When it comes time for a baby bird to
leave the nest, the parent will often push it out. We humans
frequently do the opposite and overprotect our young. Yet,

sometimes, allowing our children to experience hardship and supporting them through it can be one of the greatest gifts we can offer.

Johnny Cash wrote the hit song 'A Boy named Sue', which tells of a father who, before being imprisoned, named his newborn son Sue. The father's reasoning was that because he wouldn't be able to protect his son from within a prison, he had to provide an environment where his son would be forced to learn to protect himself.

Like hand calluses from physical labour, it's usually the things that initially seem harsh that can protect by making us stronger. I'm not advocating teasing, nor am I suggesting renaming your child with a deliberately inappropriate name. What I *am* talking about is helping your child develop resilience to life's stressors so they can learn to bounce back from hardship.

What is resilience? Resilience is a psychological term referring to a person's ability to bounce back from difficult times or recover from distress. Resilience has intrigued psychologists as to why some people can experience a setback and recover, while a similar setback may scar another person for the rest of their life. Much research has been done into the area to discover the key ingredients, and nothing destroys resilience faster than wrapping a child in cotton wool.

Cotton wool crushes confidence

Rescuing a child, as opposed to supporting them, is harmful when it comes to developing resilience. When a parent over-protects their child by trying to rescue them from normal stressors in life, the child is prevented from discovering and developing their own psychological immune system. When someone is prevented from developing their psychological immune system, they become vulnerable to both failure and mental health issues. This is because when a major difficulty does strike, and the parent can't shelter the child – failing a school exam, losing something or someone precious, or being bullied or ignored by other children – the child risks a downward mental spiral because they don't know how to cope.

Anna was in year 8, but her mother would still do everything for her. She would go through her schoolbag to check what homework had to be done, and then sit down and help Anna complete it. The thought of Anna not handing in an assignment made her mother feel sick to the stomach. Anna was not allowed out unless accompanied by an adult, which meant her mother would have to attend parties, so she chose not to go. Sleepovers were also out, as was playing any sort of sport that remotely risked injury. As a result, Anna's social skills suffered and so did her friendships at school.

This is an extreme example of overprotection, though Anna's case illustrates that if a child is deprived from experiencing their surroundings, their emotional growth is more likely to be stunted, making them vulnerable to life's multitude of stressors. Therefore it's vital for your own child's wellbeing that you start helping them develop resilience from a young age by exposing them to life's challenges.

Before you start gently pushing your child out of comfort zones, it's important to know some of the factors of resilience that allow children to bounce back from hardship. These factors include:

* **SOCIAL SUPPORT** Having a trusted person who will support, not rescue, the child by helping them through difficult times. This person's support will also involve helping the child find their own solutions to deal with the crisis at hand.

* **CHALLENGE** Resilient children see setbacks as a normal part of living, and something they can cope with. This high self-efficacy, or belief in themselves that they can cope, often allows the situation to be seen as an opportunity to learn and grow.

* **TEMPORARY AND NON-PERSONAL SITUATION** Resilient children see the problem situation as temporary and not something that will go on for the

rest of their lives. Added to this, they see the setback as a result of external factors instead of something personal about them, e.g. *I didn't win the race because the other runners were older, but next year I'll have more of a chance,* as opposed to *I fail at everything I try because I'm a loser.*

Taking the above factors into account, how can you help build resilience in your child? The first thing is to allow them to face a challenge in small, realistic steps. Remember to be positive and praise your child's successes, no matter how small.

Practical examples to help build your child's resilience levels include letting them:

* walk to school (or, if you are too far away and you drive your child, drop them off a short distance from school and let them walk)

* catch the school bus

* make their own lunch

* be responsible for doing their assignment and accepting the associated costs if they choose not to

* answer the home phone

* pay for a newspaper while you stand and watch from just outside the shop entrance.

Use the above examples as a guide only; they can help you come up with some ideas that are suitable for your child. The challenges you choose for your child will depend on their age and situation, and therefore some of the above examples may not be appropriate.

The aim of developing resilience is to let your child experience hardship in a controlled fashion so that they foster a belief in themselves that they can cope with setbacks. Your role is to prevent yourself from going immediately to their aid when they experience this mild hardship. What degree of hardship should your child be exposed to before you step in and rescue? The rule for knowing when to intervene is when the situation threatens your child's immediate safety. Otherwise stand back and allow your child to learn, which is probably the hardest thing for a parent to do.

Knowing when to stand back will be a personal judgement based on the ability of both you and your child to cope with the presenting situation. With that said, the best example I can give is when it comes to doing school homework. Be there to support but leave the ultimate responsibility of completing the homework to your child. If this means your child gets in trouble with their teacher for not completing their homework, so be it. If you rescue your child and do the homework for them, all they've learned is that when things get difficult someone will always be there to save them.

Summing up

Life isn't always smooth sailing and it does have its setbacks, but a safety blanket wrapped too tightly has its own negative consequences. Trying to shelter your child from experiencing setbacks can be extremely harmful to their ability to develop resilience. Be there to support your child, hold their hand through hard times, but let them experience the hard times instead of rescuing them. What can you do to gently push your child out of the nest, just a little?

37

KNOW YOUR OWN TROPHY CABINET

'Sadly for many children, a father is a man who expects his son to be as good as he meant to be.'

ANONYMOUS

One of the great things about having children is that you're able to experience being a child again and do things that would normally be socially unacceptable for an adult – going on swings in the playground, finger painting, singing nursery rhymes, wearing a bright children's backpack or going to see a children's movie. However, these newfound privileges come with a risk. There is an unconscious temptation for parents to try to fulfil our own needs through our children, needs that often weren't satisfied in our childhood. I call this phenomenon 'parenting trophies'.

Fiona was only ten years old, but she was fast becoming a rising star on the gymnastics circuit. Every week she and her mum would travel around the country competing in events. Even though she knew her mother was supportive of her sport, Fiona noticed that her mother would get excited if she won a competition but annoyed and sulky if she didn't. Between the long, lonely hours of training, intense competitions, strict diet and time spent travelling, Fiona lost interest. Eventually she summoned up the courage and told her mum that she'd like a break from gymnastics so she could start playing with her schoolfriends and do things they did. Fiona's request fell on deaf ears. Instead her mother said that Fiona was creating a future for herself, and that she couldn't back out now because they were so close to pre-selections for the national titles. Fiona felt trapped and helpless.

We have probably all known or heard of a child like Fiona whose parents pushed them to greatness so that the parent could feed off their success. It is easy to fall into the trap of judging these parents for craving parenting trophies. Don't be fooled! This need to experience parenting trophies through the successes of our children is a powerful motivating force that we shouldn't underestimate. Parenting trophies are fuelled by a parent's desire to have their own unmet childhood needs satisfied. These unmet needs often sprout from childhood situations where the parent felt inadequate. Examples include:

* not achieving at sport

* feeling socially unaccepted by peers at school

* doing poorly academically

* not feeling smart enough to do further study

* being seen as inferior, weak or simply uncool.

Due to these unmet childhood needs, the parent may be motivated to push their own child to succeed in the areas they didn't.

Why do parents push?

What motivates a parent to want to live their life through their child? Quite simply, acceptance from others. Whether it's money, popularity or being the best at a certain task, the need for acceptance or approval from others is often the unconscious motivation to succeed. This unconscious craving to seek others' approval is generally the driving force behind any parent's excessive desire to push their child to succeed.

Not all successes have to be big

Not all parenting trophies have to be a result of big achievements. They can also come from smaller, less obvious achievements, such as your child being able to do their homework or keep their room tidy without being asked, cook a meal, recite a funny line from a movie, do an amazing or funny trick, or get into a fight and defeat the school bully. To get the full value from a parenting trophy, the child's achievement is then mentioned by the parent to other adults at social gatherings.

To illustrate how a child's small achievement can trigger a parent's craving for a parenting trophy, I'll share an experience that a client, Trevor, had a few years ago, which still makes him cringe today. It was Christmas day and all of Trevor's family was gathered at his parents' house. His daughter was very young at the time and she was just learning to talk. Trevor tried to show a few family members how she could perform her new speech skills by singing a nursery rhyme. But his daughter didn't feel like performing; the more she resisted the more determined Trevor became. As he repeatedly sang the first lines of the nursery rhyme to his daughter without her responding, his voice got louder and louder. It wasn't long before most of the family had formed to watch her sing. The more Trevor persisted, the more uncomfortable the atmosphere became. Trevor's mother even suggested that maybe his daughter wasn't interested, but Trevor's ego was now on the line so her words were dismissed. Everyone watching laughed nervously until his daughter finally sang. The family erupted into applause, but probably more through relief that the ordeal was over. Trevor told me that the part that makes him cringe the most is that he glowed with pride after his daughter sang, as if he'd just sung the song himself and won a trophy for it.

Most of us have experienced something similar, where we've wanted to share our child's talents with others. Some parents treat their child like a pet dog and have them do tricks on command to impress others. Even though parents attain a sense of success through their child's achievements, this success will never satisfy for long.

Why parenting trophies don't last

There are two main problems with a parent trying to win parenting trophies. Firstly, the success never satisfies because it isn't experienced directly by the parent. It is like seeing a mirage while dying of thirst in the desert: you can see the water, but it's always just out of reach. The more you try to chase the mirage of meeting your own needs through your child's endeavours, the more imprisoned you become to an unattainable goal. The second problem is that a mirage is deceptive, altering a person's sense of reality. This is why a parent will feel they are pushing their child for their own good, but fail to acknowledge the real motive for pushing their child or the damage they are causing in doing so. As a result, the more they push their child to attain success, the more fractured the parent–child relationship becomes.

That's not to say that a parent can't be proud of their child in public. Nor is it to say that a parent should not encourage their child to greater things. But parents should be mindful of the motives behind why and in what area they want their child to succeed.

Rod's father, for example, was very encouraging of his son achieving at football, but nearly disowned him when he asked to take up acting lessons. It was far more acceptable for him to tell his workmates about his son's successes as a footballer than as an actor.

If expecting parenting trophies to satisfy happiness levels is an illusion and often occurs without a parent realising it, what can you do? The first step is awareness: know if you are trying to meet your own needs with your child's successes. It is so important to know your own trophy cabinet. If there are trophies you would have liked to attain as a child but didn't for whatever reason, address the issue. It's great to want to spend time with your child, but if you are doing it all to achieve a set outcome without listening to your child's wants and needs, it's likely there's a hidden motive at play.

To develop awareness of your own trophy needs, ask yourself the following questions:

* Does my child excel at a certain task and, if so, is it a task I support?

* Would I be as enthusiastic to support my child if they chose another interest to excel at, one that I don't share?

* Do I encourage my child to perform in front of others, even if they don't want to?

* Am I encouraging my child to follow a path they choose or one that I choose?

How did you go? If you were able to identify with pushing your child down a path that is more satisfying for you than for them, what can you do? The answer is to take ownership of your own trophy cabinet and aim for your own trophies. Ways this can be done include enrolling in further study, getting in shape, developing a new skill or joining a club to make new friends. If you can discover ways of experiencing your own victories in life, you will feel less of a need to pressure your own child to succeed. What's more, your child will listen more intently to your actions than your words and will be more likely to follow your example and succeed themselves.

Finally, research shows that the common thread among all childhood prodigies and children who have excelled to become adult stars is that they have a supportive and encouraging family. The trick is to make sure you encourage and support your child to follow *their* dreams, not *yours*.

Summing up

Look at your own trophy cabinet. If there are trophies missing that you never achieved as a child, resist the urge of getting these trophies through your child. Even though the allure of parenting trophies may seem tempting, it's an illusion. Unless you earn the trophy yourself, you will never be satisfied. What are your child's dreams in life, and how can you help support your child to achieve *their* dreams?

38

FIGHT IN FRONT OF YOUR CHILD

'Never doubt that a small group of thoughtful and committed citizens can change the world. Indeed it is the only thing that ever does.'

MARGARET MEAD

There is a classic saying, 'Evil happens because good people let it.' Standing up to injustice in the world, in whatever form it takes, requires tremendous courage. Why? Because few people like to rock the boat; most prefer to keep the peace. Psychological experiments have shown time and time again that we are powerfully driven to feel accepted by others, especially by those in authority. So strong is this need to be accepted by the crowd that we will even bring pain to others to achieve it.

Bob was only five, but he knew something wasn't right when his mum and her friends were all gossiping about his best friend's mum, Natasha. The women said degrading things about Natasha's fashion sense, as she had recently not been showing her usual care with her appearance. The more the women gossiped about Natasha, the more connected as a group they seemed to become. Even though Bob's mum was feeling guilty for gossiping about her good friend, she didn't stop. Bob eventually walked up and pulled on his mum's leg and said, 'Why are you saying nasty things about Charlie's mum? I thought she was your friend.' All the mothers froze, and Bob's mum felt deeply ashamed for her behaviour, especially as it was in front of her son.

Bob's intervention made the mothers stop and feel accountable for their actions, but what message had his mother given him by gossiping about her friend? Even though it's very common for people to gossip, why did she choose to continue when her guilt was telling her it was wrong?

Why don't we want to stand up to wrongdoing?

There are many reasons that people don't stand up when they see the wrong thing being done. Psychologists have discovered several psychological factors which prevent people from standing up to injustices. Some of these factors are:

* **PEER PRESSURE** Humans gain safety in numbers, so the risk of being rejected or singled out often forces a person to abide by the crowd's norms. This encourages people to keep the peace to avoid confrontation. In Bob's mum's case, having a common enemy actually brought the women closer because as long as they were gossiping about someone else, they weren't being attacked themselves. We therefore equate gossiping and bullying with deflecting a potential attack from ourselves and onto someone else. This is one reason why gossiping about others can be so enjoyable.

* **THE BYSTANDER EFFECT** This is the phenomenon that the more people present when help is needed, the less likely that any one of them will provide assistance. This is because each individual assumes that someone else will provide the help. For example, when a fire alarm goes off at work and everyone looks at each other, wondering if they should take it seriously.

* **SUBMITTING TO AUTHORITY** A classic experiment conducted in the 1960s by the psychologist Stanley

Milgram demonstrated the phenomenon that people choose to follow the orders of someone in authority, believing they are relinquishing personal accountability. For example, a manager telling an employee to do something, and the employee carrying out the orders despite believing they're wrong.

* **AVOIDING CONFRONTATION OR KEEPING THE PEACE** Some people avoid confrontation for fear of getting people offside or being labelled a trouble-maker, with the possibility of it being held against you in the future, e.g. missing out on a promotion at work because of voicing your concerns.

* **'I'M JUST ONE PERSON'** The belief that you're only one person, and that a lone person probably can't do anything anyway, e.g. standing up to a major international company because their business practices are unethical.

Can you relate to any of these barriers for standing up against injustice? We are excellent at justifying to ourselves why we didn't intervene in a situation. At times there can be a lot of truth to our reasoning, like when your physical safety is at risk by trying to stop an armed hold-up. But when the situation is just sticking to your morals and doing the right thing, even when it's uncomfortable, this is called moral courage. It can be uncomfortable doing as our morals tell us, but it can often be far worse trying to suppress them.

Why should you choose to fight for a cause in front of your child? Not only does it prevent suppressing your morals, but it also models strength and leadership to your child and gives them hope for change. Psychologists have found that a group of people can be influenced to change their minds simply by one member of the group speaking up and pointing out that what they are doing is wrong. Even though awkward, if Bob's mum had pointed out that Natasha obviously had too much on her plate to consider her clothes, it's likely the gossip would have been stopped. By taking action yourself you are teaching your child that they can make a difference and empowering them with a sense of hope.

Having a sense of hope makes children feel safer and more positive about the future when they know their parents, teachers or significant others are working to make a difference. Hope is one of the most valuable gifts we can give our children, and ourselves. Studies have shown that when it comes to the helping professions, regardless of what type of help a person seeks – whether it's a doctor, physiotherapist, teacher, nurse, naturopath or psychologist – what helps a person feel good about themselves is not always the treatment but whether the treatment or advice offers a sense of hope. Offering this sense of hope is the central tenet among all the helping professions.

If you were to fight for a cause in front of your child to model this sense of hope, what type of cause could you choose? This will be largely dependent on what is happening around you at the time, and what you feel passionate about. Feeling passionate is essential, otherwise your enthusiasm to continue fighting won't last. Keeping all this in mind, here is a short list of possible options:

* fighting to protect the environment (local or international)

* complaining to a TV station about inappropriate material being shown during children's viewing times

* lobbying council to have the local park refurbished

* organising a petition to encourage authorities to stop an injustice in the community

* supporting a person running for council who backs a particular issue you're passionate about

* phoning in to talkback radio or writing a letter to the editor of the local newspaper about a pressing issue that's being ignored by authorities.

If your child sees you fight for something you believe in, it will teach them that they can help make change even when other people do nothing. As you model hope to your child by fighting for a cause, expect to feel anxiety or discomfort. This will prepare your mind in advance so that you aren't taken by surprise. It's fear of feeling discomfort that prevents many people from taking action. However, this discomfort is generally only strong at the beginning and drops quickly.

Remember, your child will be gaining a sense of hope from your actions. I have spoken to many adults who have fiercely fought for a cause and they refer to seeing their own parents fight for a cause, which provided them with the motivation. Fighting for a legitimate cause is often empowering for both adults and children. Though, most importantly, fighting for a cause provides a sense of hope, which children thrive on.

Summing up

With global famine and pollution increasing, there is no time in history that we have needed morally courageous people to stand up against corruption and greed more. Lead by example and stand up against things in the community that you feel passionate about. That way you'll be more likely to lead others, especially your child. Be a role model and teach your child to fight for a cause; our planet depends on it.

39

FINDING THE MIDDLE GROUND ON CHANGE

'Better bend than break.'

SCOTTISH PROVERB

We don't like change at the best of times. However, children have very little control over their lives and will desperately crave that everything remains the same. When things do change and the child isn't prepared for it, it has the potential to cause all sorts of emotional problems.

Samantha was a happy, popular fifth grade student. But when she discovered that her family was moving for her father's new job, her world turned upside down. Samantha was devastated as she was given no warning about the move. She wasn't even able to say a proper goodbye to all her schoolfriends because the move happened during the school holidays. Her parents tried to console her by saying that young people naturally make new friends quickly and that it wouldn't be long before she settled in. At her new school, though, Samantha had trouble fitting in and would often spend recess and lunchtime by herself in the library. Whenever she tried bringing up her pain about the change with her parents, their awkwardness meant the conversation fell on deaf ears. Samantha could only conclude that her parents didn't love her because they took her away from her old school and town.

Change is an inevitable part of life; however, even though change can be positive, it can also be traumatic. The associated distress with change, if not handled correctly, can negatively affect a child's life.

Some common examples of change that children may experience:

* moving house

* a death in the family

* starting school for the first time or changing schools

* parents separating

* living with a parent's new partner

* a friend moving away

* a new baby in the family

* illness

* a parent losing a job or taking a new job

* new childcare arrangements, such as after-school care or a babysitter

* different financial circumstances.

When change isn't handled well, and the child isn't able to successfully process and move through the change with a sense of control, the potential for negative effects are high. Severe effects of change can trigger depression and/or anxiety in a child. This can be seen in the form of extreme clinginess, difficulties adjusting to new situations, becoming withdrawn, avoiding social situations such as school, sport or hobbies, and appearing down and not finding enjoyment in things that previously made them happy.

Even though it's more likely that severe situations of change will cause these types of emotional problems, not all situations involving change have to be as extreme as the ones mentioned. Childhood is a prime time for developing certain anxiety disorders, but many adults believe, rightly or wrongly, that children get over setbacks quickly. This belief can lead to an adult falsely seeing a very distressing situation of change for a child as a minor hiccup. Having a new teacher, joining an already established sporting team or dance class halfway through the session, losing a favourite toy and sitting in a different spot in the classroom may all seem harmless to an adult but can trigger negative reactions in children.

If your child has been through major change, would you like to help them better cope with it? If your child hasn't been through major change, would you like to help protect them against the negative effects of future change? If you answered yes to either of these questions, you may find the following strategies of interest.

The most important element in helping a child successfully deal with change is to give them back a sense of control. Remember, when a child goes through major change, not only is their world shaken but also their perceived sense of security and control. Therefore, to help your child cope with change, incorporate the three following steps into your parenting: 1) Talk about change with your child; 2) Involve your child in decisions to do with the change; and 3) Maintain familiarity in your child's life where possible. Let's take a look at these three steps in more detail.

Step 1: Talk about change with your child

Most parents fear talking with their child about a significant upcoming change, especially if the change will be upsetting for them. In an attempt to avoid upset, some parents won't tell their child about the upcoming change until the last moment. On the surface this may appear easier for the parent but it can be extremely unsettling, even terrifying, for a child, and can trigger anxiety and trust issues, such as being scared of the dark or leaving their parent. Instead, talking about change gives a child time to adjust, ask questions and be involved in finding a solution to feel better.

A great way to discuss the topic of change and show it's a normal part of life is to use the child's natural environment as a learning tool. Point out the changes that are going on around them:

* trees losing their leaves during autumn (the four seasons provide a good natural example of the cycles of change)

* the renovation or replacement of an old building

* new technology, like computers, being brought out, meaning new technical skills have to be learned (children often want the latest version of the newest technology).

Another way you can discuss change with your child is by using personal accounts. For example:

* telling stories about changes you've lived through yourself

* inviting other members of the family to tell stories about change in their lives (ensure first that their stories are child-friendly).

When telling these stories, make sure you mention your feelings about the change at the time. Talking about change will help show that it is a normal part of life, especially if you talk about your own feelings about change, as this will better assist your child to process theirs.

Step 2: Involve your child in decision-making

Naturally it will be the adults who ultimately decide the changes affecting the child. However, if a child feels like they can contribute in some way to the decision, it can help give them a sense of ownership and control over what is happening. The simple way of achieving this is compromising with your child over the less important areas of the change. For example:

* When getting rid of unused toys, for every ten toys your child donates to charity, buy them one new one (adjust this figure depending on the number of unused toys).

* Let your child choose the interior design of their bedroom walls in the new house, e.g. wall paint or posters.

* If your child chooses to accept and confront the changed situation, e.g. going to school for the remainder of the term, in spite of the new replacement teacher they don't like, give them a reward of their choosing. (*Note:* make sure the reward is realistically appropriate and not out of proportion to the situation.)

* If you are expecting a new baby, involve your child in the preparations – painting furniture, choosing items for the baby's room as well as helping choose how the room will be set up (give them a choice from your two preferred options). This involvement allows your child to feel like they still play an important role in the family.

Step 3: Maintain familiarity where possible

When children experience change, maintaining familiar objects and routines can help bring a sense of security to a new environment. Even as adults, we have our own forms of safety blankets, which bring us comfort during everyday stress. We might need to hold a handbag when out in public, or grip something, like a cup, when at a social gathering, or have a drink after work. Regardless of whether these examples are healthy, they highlight how familiar objects and routines can bring us comfort.

What are some child-friendly objects or routines you can maintain to bring comfort to your child while they are adjusting?

* If moving to a new area, find out where they can continue playing their favourite sport.

* If moving to a new house, keep their same bed or bedroom furniture (where possible) and position it in a similar way to their old room. (*Note:* Sometimes parents like to either update furniture to suit a new home or rearrange the positioning of old furniture to create a new feel. Once your child has become accustomed to the change, you can replace or rearrange the old bedroom furniture with your child's input.)

* If you are separating from your partner, now is not the time to go soft on your child and ease up on the rules. Without being a dictator, maintain the same boundaries, discipline and expectations you have always had with your child, as this familiarity will give them a sense of security.

* Eat tea at a regular time each night.

* Have a specific time for bed, which may also include a story.

*   If a child has a new teacher, tactfully ask the teacher if your child can continue to sit next to the same student in class while becoming accustomed to the change.

A note of caution, when considering anything that will bring your child comfort, make sure it helps them to deal with the anxiety instead of sheltering them from it. Don't sit them in front of a computer or TV all day or allow them to stay at home if they don't like their new relief teacher. Whatever approach you use with your child, it must build their self-efficacy to deal with the distress of change, not shelter them from it.

Summing up

Even though familiarity brings comfort, change is an inevitable part of life. Yet change can be very distressing for children, especially when they don't feel they have any understanding or control over it. Help your child better deal with change by: 1) Talking about change with them; 2) Involving your child in decisions to do with the change; and 3) Maintaining familiarity in your child's life where possible. When a child can process change in a healthy way, it allows them to move forward and continue to grow emotionally.

40

THE WEAKNESS OF NO!

'You can build a throne with bayonets,
but you can't sit on it for long.'

BORIS YELTSIN

No is a powerful word and, when used the right way, can stop a person in their tracks. This is because it not only warns against possible danger but is also a negative command which offers little direction. If you are having doubts or are unsure what I mean, try the following exercise with your child.

The Yes/No game

Mentally choose two objects in the room within close proximity to you, for example a book and a cup, without telling your child what you've chosen. Once you have your two objects, explain the rules of the game: they must locate and touch both objects, but only one at a time. You will give them feedback to help them find the objects. Here is the challenge: when trying to find the first object, you are only allowed to say the word 'No' when your child is *not* heading in the right direction. The moment they are on course towards the first object you are to remain silent. When they find the first object, they are ready to begin looking for the second object. However, for their second turn, you are only allowed to say the word 'Yes' when your child is heading in the right direction towards the second object. The moment they veer off course, you are to remain silent.

When playing this game, people usually find it more difficult to locate the hidden object when given the 'No' command than when given the 'Yes' command. Why is it that people find 'No' harder to follow than 'Yes'? By using a negative command you are telling the person what they should *not* be doing. Using a positive command tells a person what they *should* be doing. It is easier knowing what we should be doing than what we shouldn't be doing, as a negative message leaves a lot more room for uncertainty.

When a child is given a directive of what they can't do, it can create anxiety as they become unsure of what they are meant to be doing. If this situation is ongoing, they can become preoccupied with failure, fearing that if they do poorly they'll be rejected or abandoned. Ultimately, this can decrease a child's confidence and happiness levels, making them either more reserved and withdrawn or angry and defensive. Both withdrawing and acting out are common defence mechanisms children employ when they become accustomed to feeling the pain associated with being repeatedly told no.

I'm not suggesting that you can never use the word 'No' with your child. Sometimes it's warranted to say no for their own safety – 'No running on the slippery footpath', 'No talking to strangers without a parent present' and 'No playing with matches'. Even as adults, 'No' commands can be very useful: No smoking, No parking, and No entrance. My issue is not with the word no per se, but with the negative underlying message it communicates to a child when overused. These negative messages emerge when parents fall into the trap of thinking they only need to tell their child what they can't do, but forget to explain what they can do. Not only are repeated negative messages confusing for a child, but they also destroy confidence. Think back on the Yes/No game at the start of this chapter, and how confused and disorientated your child became when given the negative messages.

Don't use 'don't'

A common way parents unwittingly communicate negative messages to their child is using the word 'don't'. Overuse of the word 'don't' subtly makes a child focus on the negative message of what not to do instead of the positive directive you want to give. Take the examples shown below and imagine how the sentence would read if the word *Don't* was left out:

* Don't **WORRY ABOUT MISSING THE BALL, TOBY.**

* Don't **THINK ABOUT FAILING YOUR TEST.**

* Don't **EAT YOUR FOOD QUICKLY.**

* Don't **LOOK AT THE GROUND WHEN I'M TALKING TO YOU.**

The key for combating negative messages is instead of telling your child what they can't do, tell them what they can do. How can you achieve this?

Becoming aware of when you give your child negative messages can be hard initially. This is because negative messages are part of our everyday speech, so they become unconscious and automatic. But once you commit to noticing the way you talk to your child (and others) it won't take long before you identify the hidden negative messages in your speech.

To develop this self-awareness try the following exercise: for the next twenty-four hours notice how many times you tell your child what they can't do instead of what they can do. These negative messages could be in the form of using the word 'Don't' or a non-directional 'No'. Whenever you notice yourself giving your child a negative message, write it down. A small notebook is more convenient to carry with you. At the end of the twenty-four hours, look back on what you have written. This exercise can be eye-opening.

Remember, your goal is to first develop awareness of your use of negative messages, not to get rid of them. If you try to fight negative messages right from the start, you're likely to set yourself up for failure. This is because negative messages are often automatic, and it will take time and patience to bring them out of hiding. So your goal is just to notice when you use negative messages without being hard on yourself. The more your awareness increases, the more the negative messages will naturally decrease. Beat negative messages by noticing instead of fighting them.

Be aware of your child's messages

It's important not only to monitor if the messages you are giving your child are positive or negative, but also to help your child become aware of the directions they are giving themselves. If your child is forever telling themselves what they can't do, it's likely they will be vague about what they actually can do. This translates into low self-efficacy and shows itself in a child when they are unable to step out of a comfort zone and try something new.

Make a game out of negative messages

If your child is giving themselves negative messages, it's important to correct this. Remember, building awareness is the key. Use yourself as a role model by making a game out of raising their awareness of the negative messages of both you and your child. Whenever either of you says a negative message, to each other or yourself, the first one to identify it wins. This way you become each other's helper in raising the awareness needed for conquering negative messages. Be warned, this game is highly effective only when a parent is consistent. There may be times when you aren't in the mood to play, especially when your child is spotting your negative messages. Hold your tongue – criticising them for it will undo all the good work you've already done. If you aren't in the mood, forcing yourself to agree when your child spots your use of a negative message will show consistency, even if it means congratulating them through gritted teeth. It's this consistency that gives a child a sense of security and builds confidence.

Summing up

Parents often fall into the trap of unknowingly telling their child what they can't do instead of what they can do. These negative messages usually come in the form of *No* or *Don't*. Overuse of negative messages is destructive for your child's self-esteem. Build awareness of the use of negative messages in everyday language. It's only after this awareness is created that negative statements can be modified. What direction are your messages making your child head in?

ACKNOWLEDGEMENTS

My lovely wife Mel, thank you for your loving support. Without it, this book would never have been possible. My beautiful children, Emma and Patrick, I'm very proud to be your dad. You've both taught me so much.

My agent Sally Bird, from Calidris Literary Agency, for your tireless work and support. Fran Berry from Hardie Grant, for believing in the book and giving me this opportunity. Emma Schwarcz from Hardie Grant, you are the master of words. Once again, your amazing editing skills have refined this book and taken it to a new level. The team at Hardie Grant, your zest for your work is contagious.

Jonathan Dyer, you have been pivotal in helping me over the years with my writing career. You are a gifted writer and editor and an amazing friend.

My parents, Ron and Helen, who have always been there for me. My parents-in-law, Bruce and Cynthya, for your support, enthusiasm and love. Ian, my brother, and his wife,

Nikki, thanks for your friendship. My sister Kazz and her husband, Adrian (my brother from another mother), and my nephew Zack, for your belief in me. My brother Mick, his wife, Leanne, and my nephews Ben, Jade and Mitchell, for all your love and support. My grandmother, Marie Thorold, your strength and determination are nothing short of amazing.

David Thorold, my 'Uncle D' in New Guinea, his wife, Sal, and their daughter Sophia, thanks for your continued support. My cousins Mary Anne, Ron, Ollie and her husband, Jude, and their little son, Tonna, you're all legends!

Ron and Dee Karney, I'm forever grateful for the way you opened up your home and your lives by helping me find my way in life.

Aunty Anne, in our hearts forever.

Uncle Neil, Brent and Sarah, it's been great growing up with you.